T0346421

# The Arctic Schooner
# BOWDOIN

## 100 YEARS *of* WIND, SEA, AND ICE

KATHRYN BEALS

Down East Books

Camden, Maine

**Down East Books**

Published by Down East Books
An imprint of Globe Pequot, the trade division of
The Rowman & Littlefield Publishing Group, Inc.
4501 Forbes Blvd., Ste. 200
Lanham, MD 20706
DownEastBooks.com

Distributed by NATIONAL BOOK NETWORK

Copyright © 2022 by Kathryn Beals

*All rights reserved.* No part of this book may be reproduced in any form or by any electronic or mechanical means, including information storage and retrieval systems, without written permission from the publisher, except by a reviewer who may quote passages in a review.

ISBN 978-1-60893-764-6 (hardcover)
ISBN 978-1-60893-765-3 (e-book)

♾™ The paper used in this publication meets the minimum requirements of American National Standard for Information Sciences—Permanence of Paper for Printed Library Materials, ANSI/NISO Z39.48-1992.

*For Merlin, who was born September 27, 2010, and enjoyed his earliest months on the Atlantic at Indian Rest Lane in South Harpswell, Maine, later growing up on Spruce Head Island. He smiles whenever he sees the ocean.*

Bowdoin *to me is a monument of the finest adventure and richest experience I have ever known. She has existed to broaden man's knowledge and men's hearts, and at the same time has been a worthy tool for her Captain's teachings.*

*BOWDOIN* CREW MEMBER

# CONTENTS

# PROLOGUE

One cool morning in Southwest Harbor, Maine, I stepped aboard the S/V *Bowdoin*, docked alone at a long finger wharf at the Great Harbor Marina. She was the centerpiece of the 1995 Wooden Boat Show, a gathering of more than fifty well maintained vessels, many originally fishing or trading vessels, now often converted for education or pleasure.

Her silence is eloquent, as I am aware each time I board her. *Bowdoin* barely creaks; her communion with the wind slipping over and the water rippling beneath her is serene; her response is controlled according to the heavy oak short frames and planking of her hull, built for lifting her out of northern ice, running into "growlers," dodging icebergs, crushing pan ice, and opening and expanding leads. She is at rest in the North Atlantic on Mount Desert Island, with the unyielding weight of her substantial displacement: 66 tons. Built without a bowsprit, her waterline is less than 90 feet long.

All vessels—especially wooden vessels—speak. She whispers, murmurs, and groans, with the cracks, thuds, pops, and slap of the waves or shrieks of blowing wind against her hull. The whistling, whining, and clanking of her wooden mast, lines, and stays are gentle companions or screeching antagonists depending upon the weather gods. *Bowdoin* calmly acknowledges and asserts her presence. Designed for the heaviest weather, she is resolute and reliable, reassuring in her movements and motion underway.

I had been aboard her several times since first viewing her in the 1980s at Rockland Marine, a shipyard in the western corner of Rockland Harbor, one of Maine's largest ports. She was on the ways—a double ship railway—alongside the three-masted sovereign of the windjammers, the *Victory Chimes*. Together, the two vessels represented more than 200 years of sailing history. *Bowdoin* is to the *Chimes* as an icebreaker is to a skipjack: one a solidly built bark of exploration; the other a graceful fishing schooner.

Each time I examined her, visiting the Wooden Boat shows, then sailing in her from 2004 until the present; observing her deck replanking at the Wayfarer yard in Camden in 2017 and the final recent restoration of her hull at the Bristol Boatyard in Boothbay Harbor in 2019, she exhibited only unperturbed stability and unconditional capability. Whatever her condition, she appears ready to set sail.

When underway, the *Bowdoin* remains firmly ensconced in the sea. While most sailing vessels are lifted into the wind's realm and dance there until the sails are set, her sails seem to cleave the atmosphere, as if pushing aside the air to make way. She revels in the watery element, be it liquid, solid, or a combination.

The 88-foot vessel was created for exploration and research in the Arctic. It is appropriate that Arctic voyaging is once again becoming feasible, as *Bowdoin* celebrates her centennial and begins a new century. When she was acquired by Maine Maritime Academy in 1988, noted Captain Andy Chase first sailed the *Bowdoin* to Labrador in 1990, then above the Arctic Circle in 1991, returning her to the Arctic regions of original research, where people recognized the vessel from her earlier visits more than fifty years ago.

Captain Elliot Rappaport, the former first mate from the 1990 and 1991 voyages, returned to the Arctic with the *Bowdoin* in 1994. Her most recent Arctic voyage in 2008 was with Captain Rick Miller, a professor at Maine Maritime Academy's Transportation Department. The present master, Captain Will McLean, plans a commemorative Arctic Centennial Voyage.

The *Bowdoin* supports her legacy through her stalwart constancy. She is the base which confirms the ability to achieve a safe voyage in the ice-filled waters of the northernmost Atlantic, and exudes the eagerness to set out upon it.

How does the centennial of the S/V *Bowdoin* herald the future? If past is prologue, then this may offer some indications.

# TIMELINE OF THE S/V *BOWDOIN*

## *April 9, 1921–Present*

**APRIL 9, 1921**
Launched on April 9, 1921, at the Hodgdons Brothers Shipyard in East Boothbay, Maine.

Due to the United States Prohibition, instead of being traditionally christened, flowers were thrown over her bow by May Fogg, Donald MacMillan's niece.

**JULY 16, 1921–AUGUST 1957**
Began her first voyage down the Sheepscot River from Maine to Baffin Island, off Labrador, Canada.

Wintered over in Schooner Harbor on the southwestern coast of Baffin Island, returned to the United States the following summer.

Magnetic station established, nesting grounds of the blue goose located. Frozen in for ten months.

**1923–1924**
Wintered over in Refuge Harbor, northwestern Greenland. In September, the *Bowdoin* was "Farthest North" at 78 degrees 38 minutes, at Cape Inglefield, a world record for a 15-ton registered vessel.

Established a scientific station, took continuous meteorological and tidal observations for a year, received and sent shortwave radio messages from the United States in Morse code, placed a memorial tablet at Cape Sabine, Ellesmere Island, to honor the Greely Expedition. Frozen in for 325 days.

**1925**

Accompanied by Admiral Richard Byrd, the *Bowdoin* and an auxiliary vessel—the *Peary*, captained by George Steele—took a summer expedition to northwest Greenland to test amphibious planes beyond the Arctic Circle.

Built tidal observatory station at Etah, took color photographs of the Arctic, maintained shortwave radio contact with the U.S. mainland and naval units around the world.

**1926**

Summer expedition with the auxiliary ship *Sachem*, extensive marine life research and botanical studies at Labrador and Greenland.

**1927–1928**

Yearlong expedition with the auxiliary ship *Radio*, which returned to the United States after three months.

Scientific station established at Anetalak Bay, Labrador, and built the MacMillan Moravian School at Nain, Labrador.

Twenty-eight-foot cabin cruiser *Seeko* brought north by Captain Frank Henderson, then donated to the Moravian missionaries to facilitate their work with the Innuit.

**1929–1939**

Summer expeditions, sailing under MacMillan's command on more exploratory voyages above the Arctic Circle, exploring the deep fjords of Greenland and some of the largest and fastest moving glaciers in the world.

In 1937, instead of the *Bowdoin*, MacMillan chartered the *Gertrude Thebaud*, a larger vessel, to the Arctic, taking students with him for the first time.

**1941–1945**

*Bowdoin* purchased by the U.S. Navy, becomes the USS *Bowdoin*. First commanded by MacMillan, then continued active cartographic war work in the Arctic from 1942 to 1945 under Captain Lieutenant Stuart Hotchkiss.

Shorter Arctic voyages made under John Backland and Jack Crowell.

**1945**

Repurchased from the government and restored by MacMillan and friends of the *Bowdoin* after World War II duty. Summer expedition to Labrador for ornithological research.

**1946–1953**

Six more summer Arctic voyages conducting studies for the Hydrographic Department in Washington, DC.

Carried supplies for the Nain school; continued research in most scientific areas. MacMillan's records, left there 25 years prior in the traditional stone cairn were found by Miriam MacMillan.

**1954**
MacMillan's final Arctic expedition with the *Bowdoin*.

**1957–1969**
After eighteen successful voyages to the Arctic, the *Bowdoin* was sold to the Mystic Seaport Museum in Mystic, Connecticut, for $4,000.

Removed from the museum in 1968 and sold for $1 to the Schooner *Bowdoin* Association.

With minimal repair, sailed to MacMillan's home in Provincetown, where MacMillan saw her for the last time at the town pier in 1969.

**1970–1987**
Refit and certification as the first U.S. Sail Training Ship in 1986.

Became Maine's Official Sailing Vessel in 1986, and a U.S. Historical Landmark in 1988. She was the base for numerous successful educational voyages, lastly with Hurricane Island Outward Bound.

**1988–2008**
Sold to Maine Maritime Academy in Castine, Maine.

Sailed back to the Arctic in 1990; 150 miles above the Arctic Circle in 1991, both with Captain Andy Chase.

Sailed further past the Arctic Circle in 1994 with Captain Elliot Rappaport.

Most recent Arctic voyage in 2008 with Captain Richard Miller.

**2009–PRESENT**

Since 1989, the *Bowdoin* has been the flagship of the college's sole U.S. Sail Training Program.

Major refit including hull and deck 2017 to 2019. Endowment fund for maintenance of over $1 million established at the college.

Current master, Captain William D. McLean.

**APRIL 9, 2021**

Planning for the commemorative Arctic voyage from Castine, Maine, under Captain William McLean to celebrate The *Bowdoin's* Centennial.

# I

# AFLOAT

## In Arctic Waters

# The Birth of the *Bowdoin*

*In the choice of a ship lay the key to successful Arctic expeditions. I wanted a ship built expressly for the work, and to own her myself.*

—Donald Baxter MacMillan, 1920

MacMillan ordered ice water at the celebration for Robert Edwin Peary's 1909 discovery of the North Pole. While incomparable to the chilled Labrador water he recently siphoned off the top of a nearby iceberg a few weeks earlier, he savored its coolness nonetheless. Returning from Peary's final Arctic expedition, Donald Baxter MacMillan resolved to continue Arctic exploration. On his expedition with Peary, he had begun the research that would become his life's work.

During 1910–1920, MacMillan returned to the Arctic almost every year in an assortment of vessels, from a canoe to the 170-foot USS *Thetis*, where he served as second mate. He explored the presumed location north of Ellesmere Island of Peary's Crocker Land, which proved to be nonexistent. He retraced the steps of previous explorers, including Kane (1855), Nares (1875), and Peary himself (1906), retrieving their reports left in the customary stone cairns. After WWI Navy service testing experimental aircraft, he returned to the Arctic, joining an unsuccessful commercial voyage to Hudson Bay in 1920.[1]

After his last voyage, he returned to Freeport, Maine, and his first book, *Four Years in the White North* (Harper, 1918) was published. This book was followed by an unpublished manuscript titled *The* Bowdoin *in Baffin Land,* describing the first voyage of the schooner.[2] MacMillan received an honorary doctorate in science from Bowdoin College for his Arctic research and discoveries. He continued doctoral studies in anthropology at Harvard.[3]

While in his second teaching position at Swarthmore Preparatory School in Pennyslvania after graduating from Bowdoin College in 1888, MacMillan established a summer camp with a fellow teacher, Sam Palmer, on Bustins Island in Casco Bay. At Camp Wychmere, MacMillan taught seamanship and scientific exploration, objectives to be later advanced in 1921 with his Arctic schooner *Bowdoin,* and sustained throughout his career. The camp was very likely the first of its kind in the country, a place where boys could learn to sail a boat and study seamanship and navigation, thoroughly immersed in a marine environment.[4]

At Wychmere, MacMillan received a letter from the explorer Robert Edwin Peary, a resident of nearby Eagle Island, requesting that MacMillan privately tutor his son Robert in the subjects being taught at Camp Wychmere. Peary also inquired if MacMillan had ever considered exploring in the north. MacMillan had come to Peary's attention when he rescued ten capsized boaters on the bay over several days.[5]

MacMillan responded with thanks to Peary and described his dreams of exploring the north, asking to volunteer on Peary's expeditions. Due to teaching duties, he was unable to accompany Peary when first invited in 1907, when Peary voyaged the furthest north but did not reach his goal. However, MacMillan later accompanied

Peary in 1908 as his assistant on Peary's last voyage and the Pole's discovery.[6]

In 1921, MacMillan began teaching anthropology at Bowdoin College, although he still longed to revisit the Arctic. While planning his return, he concluded that "in the choice of a ship lay the key to successful Arctic exploration."[7] Furthermore, MacMillan wanted a ship "built expressly for the work, and [to] own her himself."[8] His own practicality, along with Peary's advice that "hiring a ship at $15,000 is what consumes valuable funds that should be used for other purposes," influenced his decision.[9]

Earlier Arctic explorers Dr. Elisha Kent Kane and Dr. Isaac Israel Hayes had successfully voyaged in the 1800s with small sailing ships. Sails, with the minimal use of auxiliary power, both reduced the amount of necessary fuel and its cost, as well as offered additional funds and space for supplies. The larger, heavier, metal ships were often icebound, or irreparably damaged, whereas small, wooden ships had the size and commensurate flexibility to maneuver and withstand Arctic conditions.[10]

Indeed, a sailing vessel of 55 tons in 1616, the *Discovery*, was one of the first to sail in Arctic waters. While this is easily acknowledged by those who have seen authentic replicas of Christopher Columbus's ships, nevertheless, allegedly due to her small size, the claim and reports of her important discovery of only water at the North Pole were disregarded for over 200 years.[11]

With his knowledge of Arctic conditions, MacMillan envisioned a vessel able to travel within the ice, offer adequate protection for herself and her crew, and carry the supplies required to not only survive but to safely research, work, live, and connect with native Inuit, fishermen, Moravian missionaries, and fur traders inhabiting the Arctic. As fuel was usually unavailable north of Sidney, Nova Scotia, the ship must be minimally powered, with an engine able to burn a combination of kerosene, whale and seal oil if needed. Moreover, a small vessel could be buried in the snow to protect her from the climate.[12]

MacMillan described the requirements for his vessel:

*She should be of wood, and not one whit larger than is necessary to carry the equipment and provisions of the personnel, plus the quality of seaworthiness in sailing the waters en route to the objective point. Theoretically, a small ship can be constructed stronger than a large one. She will lift more easily when under pressure, she can worm herself through narrow leads, she can take sharper corners, she can hug the land for safety, take refuge from the pack behind rocks and ledges, anchor in shallow harbors, and when frozen in can be more easily and quickly banked with snow and more economically heated. She should have the very best of a white oak frame, heavy oak planks, white pine decks, a heavy ceiling of Oregon pine, and an outside sheathing of greenheart or ironwood to serve as a protection against the abrasive power of ice. To be without this last . . . is to court disaster from the minute one enters the ice.*[13]

Importantly, since the Arctic tides were slightly more than 10 feet, the ship would draw only 10 feet to be capable of sailing close to shore, where the ice was thinner. Furthermore, she could be bottomed out at high tide to accomplish any maintenance or needed repairs, then refloated at the next high tide.[14]

MacMillan had read of the Norwegian explorer Fritijof Nansen's ship *Fram*, which was deliberately frozen in the ice pack. The 127-foot ship had floated for three years, coming within 273 miles of the North Pole; its rounded hull preventing the ice pressure from crushing the vessel. Nansen had taken soundings during the voyage, finding that the ocean north of Siberia was over 2 miles deep, proving to most that there was not a large landmass near the pole. MacMillan wrote "that the staunch Fram ever came back was almost a miracle."[15] Subsequently, a rounded hull became part of his design.

The rounded hull would be narrow and deep, allowing her to be thrust above the ice when she became icebound, be righted when freed by the incoming tide. To direct the flow of ice away from the stern and vulnerable propeller, the hull's width of 21 feet would be greatest just aft of amidships rather than immediately forward. The engine drives a single screw, protected by a skeg that runs from keel to rudder.[16]

For additional safety, MacMillan planned two watertight bulkheads so that both ends of the vessel would float, even if she was broken in half. This was later adapted for its fail-safe properties, and presently, the *Bowdoin* has five watertight compartments.[17]

All this would necessitate a sturdy wooden construction, so grounding on the bottom or hitting ice floes would not do other than minimal damage, to be repaired with a new plank or two. With these requirements, MacMillan commissioned well-known marine architect William H. Hand of New Bedford, Massachusetts, to design a schooner. Furthermore, Hand agreed with naval architect John Alden on the choice of a shipyard, who said, "If I could get them, I'd never let anyone but the Hodgdon brothers of East Boothbay touch a ship of mine."[18]

After meeting with the Hodgdons, and agreeing upon a cost of $35,000, MacMillan's Artic exploration vessel began assembly at the Hodgdon Brothers Shipyard in East Boothbay, Maine. The yard was later sold to Joel Stevens and Jake Goudy, who carefully maintained the *Bowdoin* through the years for MacMillan using the originally specified materials for all maintenance and repairs. While Hand had drawn the basic design, Charles Hodgdon supplemented the double hull, reinforcing with white oak, the last treenailed vessel Hodgdons built.[19]

MacMillan named his vessel after Bowdoin College, from which he graduated in 1898, delayed a year due to illness. At the *Bowdoin*'s dedication, MacMillan's niece, May Fogg, was unable to break the traditional bottle of champagne over her bow due to Prohibiton. Instead, May recalls, "I stood in the bow, with Uncle Don right next to me, and I threw flowers overboard."[20]

The *Bowdoin* is a gaff-rigged knockabout schooner with two Douglas fir masts, a white oak hull, and white pine deck. Reinforced with white oak for Arctic conditions and originally sheathed with iron-wood up to the waterline, she carries an observation barrel at the top of her foremast.

The *Bowdoin* was first built with a 60-horsepower Fairbanks Morse engine, capable of burning crude oil, kerosene, and even seal or whale oil if necessary. Using 120 gallons a day, or 5 gallons an hour, allowed a motor cruising speed of 8 knots, with a radius of 3,629 miles, although the *Bowdoin* is only 15 tons net with a 2,200-gallon tank capacity.[21] This was replaced with a Cummins 100 HP Diesel as a gift from Cummins, and she is presently powered by a 190 HP Cummins Diesel.[22]

MacMillan believed that when "navigating in such dangerous waters, a ship should have the double margin of safety by being well equipped with both sails and power, for rapidly whirling propeller blades in contact with ice are easily bent and stripped, and shafts broken."[23]

At the time the *Bowdoin* was built, "she was the strongest wooden vessel in the world. She aroused the admiration of everybody who worked on her, and since then of everybody who sailed aboard her."[24]

Comparable admiration of her continues. In the present day, she is an established sight along the shores of Maine, serving not only as a college training ship but as a goodwill ambassador, the Official Maine State Vessel.

The *Bowdoin* first became a recognizable feature in another part of North America, as she sailed eighteen voyages for MacMillan's expeditions exploring the Arctic from 1921 to 1954.[25] MacMillan's earliest voyages were made with only the aid of frequently inaccurate charts—which he corrected through research and observation—with only a fathometer to read depth and a radio direction finder to determine his location. However, on her last voyage in 1954 with MacMillan, *Bowdoin* carried the latest communication and navigation equipment, flying the flag for MacMillan's new rank of rear admiral from the mainmast.[26]

MacMillan's first voyage in 1921 with his new ship was to Baffin Island, north of Labrador. Baffin Island was found in 1616 by Robert Bylot, the master of the ship *Discovery,* one of the first ships to sail in the Arctic region. The sighting was credited to his pilot, a historian who wrote about the discovery, and signed the information: *Written by William Baffin.* The captain's only recognition was from the naming of an island off the northern coast of Baffin Island as Bylot Island.[27]

MacMillan additionally planned to explore the unknown eastern side of the island to answer one of ornithology's unsolved problems: locating the breeding grounds of the blue goose. He determined that the breeding grounds of the goose were in the interior of Baffin Island, and although the schooner did not sail to the eastern side, eventually a nest with a clutch of eggs, obtained by an Innuit, was brought back by a crew member.[28]

The Carnegie Institution in Washington, DC, donated supplies with which MacMillan and crew, including Navy Ensign Richard Goddard of Winthrop, Massachusetts, later a professor of astronomy at Dartmouth College, built at Schooner Harbor, where the *Bowdoin* was moored for the winter. It was one of many scientific stations for the study of Northern terrestrial magnetism and atmospheric electricity that were established due to the many magnetic fluctuations found in the region.[29]

Leaving Wiscasset, Maine, down the Sheepscot River on July 16, the *Bowdoin's* six-man crew was composed of scientists. Mac-Millan relied on the universities, geographic societies, and natural history museums to help fund his expeditions; in payment he conducted research for them.

MacMillan had paid for the *Bowdoin's* construction partly through his lectures, as well as publishing articles and photographs in *National Geographic* magazine, although most of the schooner's cost had been met by selling $100 shares in her to people interested in science. His second book, the first published on his own expeditions, *Etah and Beyond, or Life Within Twelve Degrees of the Pole*, is dedicated to "My good friends who helped me build the *Bowdoin* and thus made my Arctic work possible."[30]

Above the coast of Labrador, the *Bowdoin* entered the Hudson Strait at Port Burwell and continued up the western coast of Baffin Island, around the Foxe Basin, crossing and recrossing the Arctic Circle near Cape Burnil. MacMillan wrote that the Arctic Circle was an "imaginary line, called by the ancient Greeks the 'Bear's Circle,' hence our name, 'Arctic,' from the Greek word meaning bear. A circle drawn through the constellation of the Great Bear was the limit of the stars always visible to the Greeks above the northern horizon."[31]

On August 23, the *Bowdoin* was above the Arctic Circle, with no northern or western openings in the surrounding icepack. Instead of backing up to a glacial freshwater stream feeding into the ocean, they tied onto pan ice, and filled their water tanks from the pool of fresh water always on the surface of the floe, then headed out under power to the southeast. MacMillan searched in this direction and found open water after hours of navigation, then headed northeast under sail. MacMillan kept watch in the ice barrel that served as a crow's nest 60 feet above the deck, while the botanist Rutherford Platt was at the helm.[32]

Unexpectedly, a growler—an old, compacted iceberg—abruptly appeared. Unable to avoid it, the *Bowdoin* struck it at the center. However, MacMillan wrote, "the *Bowdoin* bounded like a rubber ball, and went serenely on her way, but for the rest of the night at reduced speed. She had had her baptism by fire and emerged triumphant."[33]

Near Cape Dorset, they rounded King Charles Cape later that week and discovered a large island with a substantial deep-water harbor, an ideal sanctuary safe from winds from any direction. With sufficient depth at low water, freedom from ice pressure and strong currents, abundant game, and a good water supply, here the *Bowdoin* would remain for the winter. The port became known as Schooner Harbor and is still designated by this name on the charts.[34]

When the Canadian government later proposed that Schooner Harbor be renamed Bowdoin Harbor, MacMillan requested a different site. He named a small harbor in northern Labrador—near the dangerous area of Cape Chidley—Bowdoin Harbor, to commemorate his vessel. Bowdoin Harbor is now on the Labrador charts MacMillan helped edit from 1943 to 1945.[35]

To prepare for the winter, MacMillan's crew dismantled all of the running rigging and set the strongest anchor into the prevailing winds as best could be determined, running a line from the stern to a beach rock. They removed all the cargo, provisions, and camping gear to the shore, building living quarters and a shed for atmospheric and magnetic measurements above the high-water mark in case of a fire, which had occurred with many expedition ships, including Peary's. With snow blocks packed around her for insulation, and igloos built around her hatches, by October 10, the schooner was frozen in for the winter.[36]

The men's winter activities included hunting—both for exercise and supplementing their provisions—monitoring the recording machines for measurements, weather and sky research, and exploring the area. As always, MacMillan spent a great deal of time studying the sky:

*An Arctic winter can never be monotonous to one interested in astronomy, for nowhere is there more beautifully displayed than in the North sun pillars, parhelia, paraselenae, halos, coronae, glories, mirage, looming, fata morgana, and purple lights.*[37]

The native Innuit became companions and guides, hunting and fishing, building, sewing clothing, exploring, and working.

*They have no watches to tell them when to get up, when to go to bed, when to eat, when to do everything; watches weren't necessary. The first magnitude star, known to us as Arcturus, tells them all. It revolves in the sky and tells them how long they have been traveling, how long they have slept. And when the stars have gone to rest, the sun, revolving in the sky, tells them all they need to know.*[38]

By July 2, with the warmest temperatures approaching, the crew of the *Bowdoin* prepared to leave. Although the harbor ice remained more than 4 feet thick, they sprinkled coals from the stove and sand from the beach around the ship for 30 yards ahead of the schooner out to the anchor. The sun warmed the sand and melted the ice. In three weeks a channel appeared.[39]

The anchor was weighed, and *Bowdoin* motored ahead, to be beached by the harbor's entrance. There the ice damage to the propeller was repaired, she was securely closed up, and righted herself on the returning high water. The schooner floated off as designed and was underway. Architect Billy Hand had done his work well.[40]

The next morning, they began the voyage home. To save time, MacMillan wanted to go through McLelan Strait, an 8-mile-long fjord directly through Cape Chidley. Difficult to navigate unless the tide is high, nevertheless,

> *the* Bowdoin *came through beautifully, once she found the door, and bowed gracefully to the heavy swell rolling into the mouth of the run from the outside ledges white with surf. Under sail we skimmed along the shore on the inside run close under the snow-capped mountains of one of the most awe inspiring and striking bits of scenery in North America.*[41]

Finally, on September 9, they were sailing along the Nova Scotia coast, and the sky was so clear that seven navigational lights could be seen at one time, some well beyond theoretical range. But the next day was fogged in as the schooner headed to Monhegan Island and arrived early. She spent the night there and continued on to Boothbay the next day, where the customary large crowd of well-wishers welcomed her.[42]

The new schooner had proved her worth and borne out Mac's theories on what an Artic vessel should be by successfully wintering in the ice, and being the first ship to circumnavigate the difficult Foxe Basin.[43] The *Bowdoin*'s characteristic dependability had been demonstrated, and it would not be the only time.

## 2

# The Arctic Expeditions

*As the daylight faded, the breeze freshened. This is what* Bow-doin *liked. The old girl picked up her skirts and reeled off the knots. The sea built up and crested with foam that gleamed white in the starlit night. The vessel would run down one sea and swing up as the next one lifted her transom as the cycle was repeated. The action was rhythmic as one sea followed the other.*
—Captain Stuart Hotchkiss, 1942

On June 23, 1923, the Bowdoin sailed north again for 15 months from Wiscasset, Maine. She left three days later from the island of Monhegan off the coast of Maine at 3:45 p.m., laying a 120-degree course for a lighted buoy 5 miles south of Seal Island, Nova Scotia.[1]

However, the *Bowdoin's* compasses were completely reversed when she experienced an electrical storm off Nova Scotia. Mac-Millan headed mistakenly for West Head Light on the western shores of Cape Sable and was forced to retrace her route. MacMillan's admonition was to "make dead sure of your light or landmark. A positive identification of such is far more valuable than lead, log, or compass course."[2]

Eventually arriving August 6, 1923, at Cape York, Greenland, about 11:00 a.m., they anchored off Etah, though chose on August 17 to winter slightly farther north at Refuge Harbor. Four fathoms of water were within 50 feet of the low-water mark, so the *Bowdoin* could lie close to the beach, and MacMillan found that "all the conditions are so ideal."[3] Additionally, Dr. Elisha Kent Kane had wintered there seventy years ago.

MacMillan wrote in the preface of *Etah And Beyond,* his second book:

> *The* Bowdoin, *built especially for Arctic work, had returned from her maiden trip. She had proven quite conclusively that a small wooden ship of the right model and right construction is in many ways better than a steel ship. She had penetrated successfully the ice packed waters of the Foxe Channel, had gone beyond the Spicer Islands, had cruised along the west coast of Baffin Land, the first exploration ship since two hundred years ago. After being frozen in the ice for three hundred and six days, she was ready for her second trip. . . . The* Bowdoin *and her crew are once more ready to sail from Wiscasset, in the hope of bringing back the results of new discoveries and observations that shall add something worthwhile to the sum of human knowledge.*[4]

Two institutions sponsored the expedition. The Carnegie Institution requested more information about Greenland's magnetic field, as MacMillan had gathered about Baffin Land on the *Bowdoin's* initial voyage. The explorer wrote about the schooner's second voyage:

> *The purpose of the expedition was to establish as many new magnetic stations as possible, and also to reoccupy former stations.*

*. . . The results derived from such study are of great value to ascertaining the horizontal and vertical intensity of the earth's magnetism. . . . Very little work of this character has been attempted in the Far North.*[5]

Additionally, the National Geographic Society sent a memorial tablet for the Greely Expedition to be placed at their last camp on Cape Sabine on Ellesmere Island.[6]

MacMillan flew the *Bowdoin*'s flag at half-mast when he learned of President Harding's death in August; *Bowdoin*'s flag was the northernmost flag honoring the late president. By early October, the harbor had frozen over. As they had done on Baffin Island, snow blocks were packed around the schooner, and igloos were built around the hatches for insulation.[7] The *Bowdoin* was frozen in again through the winter.

The U.S. Weather Bureau supplied equipment to record the temperature, barometric pressure, snow accumulation, humidity, and wind conditions—45.3 degrees below zero was recorded in February. The men continued glacier and magnetic research and built a cairn to record the schooner's sojourn there. On April 6, MacMillan raised the *Bowdoin*'s flag to celebrate the anniversary of the North Pole's discovery.[8] In early May, MacMillan decided to travel via dogsled to Cape Sabine to install the Greely Memorial tablet, and it was dedicated on May 8 in honor of the men who had perished there waiting for rescue.[9]

In July, noting that the thick harbor ice had not melted, MacMillan's crew began sawing chunks of ice around the *Bowdoin*. Eventually she was freed but sailed less than 100 yards and became grounded at high tide on an underwater ledge. As the tide ebbed, she fell on her port side, crashing into the water over her rail, and breaking several planks on her hull. However, after unloading supplies to lighten her, sealing up her hatches, as well as caulking any openings, she refloated two tides later, and was found to be seaworthy.[10]

Attempting to leave, she was blocked at the harbor's entrance by an iceberg pressing firmly against the shore on the starboard side. There appeared to be some leeway on the port side. Only part of the harbor wall's

> *'old winter ice' impinged against the berg—if the* Bowdoin *could just crack that ice and shove it to one side. . . . MacMillan backed the schooner to the end of the channel. . . . First at half, then at full speed, the schooner charged down upon the "ice gate . . . ."[Striking the gate] the* Bowdoin, *all sixty tons of her, stopped short and everything aboard, animate and inanimate, went skittering forward in a heap.*
>
> *McMillan went forward to inspect damage, and found, to his great relief, that her steel shod oak stem was not even dented, but that wiggling away from her bow was a crack through the middle of the pan ice.*
>
> *The little schooner leaned into that crack, churning up a magnificent wake with her efforts, opened it up a yard, then two, and finally wide enough to squeeze through. To windward the berg pressed threateningly against the pan, but with full speed ahead, they shot out into open water, a strong southwesterly and heavy sea, bound for home, the* Bowdoin *slightly battle scarred but totally unvanquished.*[11]

Admiral Peary, honored as the discoverer of the North Pole, accurately predicted in 1924 the conquest of the North and South Poles by airplane.[12] MacMillan aided in this transition on his next voyage. Returning to Greenland a year later in 1925, the expedition was sponsored by the National Geographic Society, in conjunction with the U.S. Navy. The *Bowdoin* was the flagship, and a larger vessel, the SS *Peary*, carried the parts of three amphibious biplanes.

The Arctic summer had been colder than usual, with increased ice in the water. On the voyage, the *Bowdoin*'s propeller broke and was replaced, and the *Peary* ran aground and was refloated. Both ships were icebound in Melville Bay, in "the real pack-hard blue ice five feet thick," confirmed MacMillan, who ordered the expedition—including Commander Richard E. Byrd—to wait for the ice to clear.[13]

Eventually Refuge Harbor and Etah was reached, and the planes were assembled and began test flights. They were unable to explore the area over the polar sea, as the planes could not land, due to the uneven ground, for refueling. Aerial photographs were made, as well as notes about upper air wind currents and temperatures, which MacMillan hoped would assist in the study of meteorological conditions and weather forecasts.[14]

MacMillan succeeded in transmitting voice messages, rather than Morse Code, over the radio. His first message was received by the USS *Seattle* off the Tasmanian coast in Australia. Subsequently, messages from family, concerts, and speeches were enjoyed. President Calvin Coolidge sent Christmas greetings. Shortwave radio voice contact was again used when the *Bowdoin* and the *Peary* were separated in pack ice on the voyage home, which helped to establish the Navy's long-distance fleet communications.[15]

The short Arctic summer ended, and the *Bowdoin* sailed for home with the *Peary*. MacMillan had acknowledged that, despite difficulties, aviators would dominate polar exploration. The next spring, Richard Byrd and Floyd Bennett flew over the North Pole, and confirmed that only ice existed at the top of the earth.[16]

Now, planes easily flew into all areas of the North, established a base, and with a supply source, began exploration for as long as was needed. Nevertheless, the *Bowdoin* still had a valid reason to continue; as MacMillan stated earlier in his second book, "We have passed by and neglected at our very doors lands rich in beauty and in scientific facts."[17] However, *Bowdoin*'s mission changed from discovery and exploration to education and public relations.

In 1926, shortly after the polar sea had been examined from the sky, MacMillan set sail in the *Bowdoin*, accompanied by the auxiliary yacht *Sachem*, to resume scientific studies. He remembered the discovery of coal and plant fossils in the high Arctic. Large coal deposits existing on Disko Island and elsewhere were proof that the ice had melted and the Arctic had warmed in an earlier age, and he believed this would reoccur. The Field Museum of Chicago had again sponsored this summer expedition, and many plants were collected for study. As well, further research was conducted on marine life.[18]

MacMillan sailed the *Bowdoin* up the Labrador coast, bumping into reefs and ice floes, taking many soundings, and finding new danger areas, constantly revising the navigational charts. He sent the schooner into ice fields and wedged her through, splitting the ice. He rammed her reinforced bow up onto the ice and cracked the ice open with her weight. The ship cut through with the "engine at full speed and vibrating from keel to ice barrel."[19] In his unpublished manuscript, MacMillan stated:

> *In navigating unknown waters, a rough sea is always preferable for this reason—it never fails to reveal its own dangers. Where white water cannot be seen, it is safe for the* Bowdoin *of ten-foot draft to hold her course.*[20]

From the schooner, he took many photos of the hundreds of icebergs, able to see as many as 125 at one time; and he made a movie, *Eskimo Life in South Greenland.* On his return in March 1927, his second book, *Etah and Beyond*, was published, and he received the Elisha Kent Kane Medal from the Explorer's Club, for "daring exploration and scientific research."[21]

On each expedition, MacMillan brought scientists from more than a dozen colleges and universities, whose research and observations, including his own work, contributed to the fields of oceanography, meteorology, glaciology, archeology, paleontology, anthropology, geology, geography, biology, botany, zoology, seismology, ornithology, and ichthyology.[22]

Dr. Gilbert Grosvenor of the National Geographic Society wrote in his foreword for *Etah and Beyond:*

> *With only one or two exceptions, each succeeding season has seen him hard at work in that region. Enriching the world's knowledge of its geography and geology, gathering meteorological data and biological information, and laying the foundation upon which future Arctic research will largely rest. . . . It is truly a wonderful experience to sail with him on his* Bowdoin, *and watch the amazing dexterity with which he handles the little vessel in all kinds of weather.*[23]

In June 1928, MacMillan sailed the *Bowdoin* on another expedition north, with plans to winter in Nain, Labrador. The Field Museum of Chicago had again sponsored his voyage, and after their arrival in Nain, the first mate of the *Bowdoin,* Jack Crowell, took the schooner north to Frobisher Bay on Baffin Island to collect fossils. MacMillan remained in Nain on an accompanying auxiliary ship brought north, the *Radio.* She was less suitable for heavy weather and Arctic conditions and returned south after three months.[24]

At Nain, he began to study another native ethnic group, the Naskapi Innu, as he had first recorded the language and lifestyle of Greenland's Inughuit and Canada's Inuit. Later, improving the lives of the natives of Nain, MacMillan gave them the inventions of radio, electricity, a snowmobile, and a small motor vessel, the *Seeko*. Next, he built a school, and on the *Bowdoin*'s voyage north in 1929 brought all the supplies needed, obtained through the aid of the *Bowdoin*'s many supporters and friends.[25]

After unloading his supplies at Nain, MacMillan returned to Baffin Island to study fish. In an icy rain, he moored the *Bowdoin* on an ice anchor set in an iceberg in Frobisher Bay. Suddenly, the ice anchor pulled out as the schooner creaked under the strain of a strong current. It was caused by the approach of a huge iceberg. The *Bowdoin* was caught between the iceberg behind her and the mountain of ice bearing down on her.

In the ice barrel observation post 60 feet above the deck, Mac-Millan shouted commands: "Hard-a-port!" Then: "Hard to starboard!" The helmsman struggled to obey and kept a little open water between the ship and the icebergs as a buffer, hoping the schooner would not be crushed. It worked; the schooner squeaked as she was scraped amidships by the gigantic berg as it floated past, but she was safe.[26]

After returning home, he planned another expedition for the summer of 1930. The United States was in an economic depression, and MacMillan engaged a different crew—college students, who paid to accompany him north, earning academic credit. On this voyage, they explored the areas where Viking ruins had been discovered. The *Bowdoin* sailed throughout the northern islands: to Iceland, Greenland, Baffin Island, Labrador, and Newfoundland—over

8,000 miles—and the students returned as competent sailors and experienced explorers.[27] MacMillan had been interested in educating others in the ways of the sea since his teaching days. Now he expanded this program, and ultimately it became the *Bowdoin*'s present mission.

All Arctic expeditions experienced the severe climate, as the weather created challenging events for all the vessels going north, and the *Bowdoin* was not spared. On MacMillan's fourteenth expedition in 1931, he flew to Labrador from Maine, while his first mate, Jack Crowell, sailed the *Bowdoin* on her eighth northern voyage.[28]

MacMillan was recognized as an expert in Labrador coast navigation, and the British government asked him to take aerial photographs and identify the many submerged features of the sea in the Nain area, known to be dangerous to sailing vessels. He took thousands of photographs and realized that he needed the help of an assistant. [29]

Moreover, MacMillan had just begun as a visiting professor of anthropology at Bowdoin, and published his third book, *Kahda: Life of a North Greenland Eskimo Boy.* He was also completing his fourth book, *How Peary Reached the Pole: The Personal Story of His Assistant,* which was intended to acknowledge the black explorer Mathew Hensen, the only person with Peary at the Pole, and settle the questions raised about Peary's discovery.

Additionally, MacMillan needed to raise funds. As usual, letters needed to be typed to solicit money for the Nain boarding school, secure sponsors for the *Bowdoin*'s future expeditions, and arrange lecture tours as well as narrating his movies being shown across the United States. Photographs and specimens needed to be cataloged, and details for the next expedition needed to be planned.

Jerry Look, an old friend and supporter, had, along with his daughter, Miriam, followed MacMillan's career. She often attended the *Bowdoin*'s voyage embarkments and return celebrations attended by thousands of well-wishers and sent him letters; he had brought her gifts from his voyages. She left another position in public relations and accepted his offer to work on his collections. She said she became "so involved in Arctic lore that I got the wild idea of going North myself."[30]

In 1934, he sailed the *Bowdoin* north for the summer, stating in a newspaper article, "I just can't stay away from the snows and floes for long."[31] Bowdoin College and Clark University sponsored the voyage, and again, the crew were mostly college students with a few scientists.

Ornithology was the focus of research, and in Labrador, the crew banded several hundred Arctic terns—which flew each year down to Antarctica and back—to learn their annual migration route. Three crew members were left in north Greenland to study plant life, returning with more than 20,000 plants. In the Button Islands, six more crew stayed to study the bird population, seeing thousands of birds.

Leaving a dory for the men to use if the schooner could not make the shore, the *Bowdoin* had to leave the islands, as the strong currents there swept ice constantly into her path, along with thick fog and frequent storms, and the 30-foot tides made sailing treacherous. Farther along the coast, MacMillan found a small protected inlet among the cliffs. This he named Bowdoin Harbor.[32]

Another successful exploration had been completed, and MacMillan returned to Maine. In March 1935, he married Miriam Look near St. Augustine, Florida. He was 60; she was 29; they settled back in Provincetown, in his boyhood home.[36] Eventually Miriam was able to accompany him on his voyages on the *Bowdoin*.

She authored her own book, published in 1948. She wrote in *Green Seas and White Ice:*

> *My greatest thrill of the entire trip was steering the* Bowdoin *through the ice-jammed waters of Smith Sound and on into Kane Basin within 660 miles of the North Pole. . . . I thank the* Bowdoin *for getting me there and getting me back.*[33]

In 1938, the *Bowdoin* remained in Maine, and MacMillan chartered the *Gertrude L. Thebaud* so that more scientists and students could join him. This was the first formal beginning of instructing youth in seamanship, navigation, and Arctic knowledge, supplanting exploration as the primary reason for the *Bowdoin's* voyages.

The *Bowdoin* sailed north again in 1939, along with a dozen high school and college students. They recorded the distance covered by a fast-moving glacier and explored the deep fjords of Greenland. Returning home, the *Bowdoin* was stopped and inspected by a patrol boat in September when they entered Sydney, Nova Scotia. Germany had just invaded Poland, and Great Britain and France had declared war.[34]

World War II had begun in Europe, and Greenland belonged to Denmark, which had been invaded by Germany. In 1940, MacMillan had to cancel his summer expedition, since he had not received the required permits from Denmark. In 1941, MacMillan's plans for the voyage north were again cancelled, as he had received an offer to charter the *Bowdoin* for $1,000 a month by the U.S. Army. However, MacMillan was a retired Naval Reserve officer, and he wanted to consult with the Navy before deciding.[35]

MacMillan visited Washington, where an admiral proposed that the *Bowdoin* be sold to the Navy. MacMillan would remain as her captain. Although MacMillan was 66 years old, as a reserve officer, he could be called to duty at any time, and America was soon to go to war. As one of the best northern sea navigators, MacMillan and his ship would help to defend the North American coast.

His decision was inconsequential; the Navy had earlier sent officers to Maine to survey the schooner and offered $50,000 to buy her. Furthermore, MacMillan's orders had also been sent. So, in 1941, MacMillan commanded the USS *Bowdoin* to Greenland, where he would survey fjords for the Navy Hydrographic Office and make plans to establish two military airfields.[36]

However, in February 1942, MacMillan received orders to return to active duty in Washington, DC, as a consultant to provide accurate charts of the Northeast coast, considered a strategic area. His orders separated him from his ship. *Bowdoin* was painted with blue and white camouflage, with the number "50" on both sides of the bow, designating her as *IX-50, Miscellaneous Vessel*, and antiaircraft guns were mounted on her forward decks.[37]

In 1942, she was first captained by a young Navy officer, Yale graduate Lt. Stuart Hotchkiss, described as "a man who knows sail." Hotchkiss was an experienced ocean racer and had won the 1935 Fastnet Race aboard the yacht *Stormy Weather*.[38]

After examining the schooner on the marine railway, Hotchkiss ordered repairs and new equipment. The rot around the rigging eyes and in a large section of the inner three of the five aprons strengthening her stern were repaired, and an electric air compressor and a 7.5-kilowatt generator were installed to start the Fairbanks-Morse diesel. An auxiliary generator, a Sperry Gyro compass, and an oil-fired space heating boiler completed the necessary updates.

With the new equipment in place, the *Bowdoin* became heavy at the bow. To trim the schooner, 1,000 pounds of lead was needed. This was installed after rejecting several commanders' suggestions to move the two 500-pound anchors aft, since moving these would create difficulties in getting underway and anchoring.[39]

Hotchkiss sailed the *Bowdoin* all the way to Greenland without using power.[40] They left Boston on May 4, arriving in Greenland at the Coast Guard Greenland Patrol Station at Sondrestrom on May 21. Their mission was to conduct hydrographic surveys of the fjord, which is over the Arctic Circle, then move 300 miles south to do the same at Narsarsursak. At Sondrestrom, there were few soundings marked, and they sailed along the inland passage marked by a route line. The *Bowdoin* would return fifteen months later to survey and chart the area under another skipper.[41]

Going north, they had days of good sailing and slow days due to the weather. Hotchkiss wrote that "on a broad reach, the entire rig would surge forward as the schooner slid down the back of a wave," and he worried about its strength.[42] Three days out from Greenland, the main gaff snapped. Reaching Sondrestrom, the gaff was repaired, and running backstays were installed to additionally support the mainmast. Returning home in September, Hotchkiss wrote of the voyage:

> As the daylight faded, the breeze freshened. This was what Bowdoin *liked. The old girl picked up her skirts and reeled off the knots. The sea built up and crested with foam that gleamed white in the starlit night. The vessel would run down one sea and swing up as the next one lifted her transom as the cycle was repeated. The action was rhythmic as one sea followed the other.*[43]

Due to the Greenland coast's magnetic variation and declination of over 50 degrees, the compass card revolved in its bowl because the horizontal force was so weak. Hotchkiss noted, "It's a little distracting when the compass card starts rotating like a roulette wheel."[44] However, they also had the gyro compass to verify direction.

He noted the *Bowdoin*'s qualities again when the winds increased to a gale:

*As she came up amid the roar of flapping canvas she took a heavy sea across the starboard rail and rolled deeply to leeward burying her lee deck. . . . We were doing about eleven knots at the time.*

*That night I was again impressed by one of the* Bowdoin's *qualities. The wind and seas could roar on deck but down below in the after cabin she seemed as silent and steady as a church.*[45]

Noticing one morning in the fjord at Narsarsusak when the schooner was pushing through quarter-inch glazed ice that "the thin ice was cutting through like a knife into her oak planking," Hotchkiss stopped and installed protective sheathing. Radioing the base, a steel hulled trawler brought out galvanized sheet iron and boat nails, along with 2 x 10 planking. Anchored in a nearby harbor and heeled over with the main boom swung over the side, the sheathing was installed by circling the *Bowdoin* in a dory.[46]

In November, the engine seized up, and they sailed to the base for a major overhaul. Traces of the settlement established by Erik the Red in the tenth century could be seen directly across from the airbase. Hotchkiss wrote this graceful description of the *Bowdoin*'s prowess:

*That night it snowed hard, but early in the morning the storm passed leaving us with six inches of snow on deck, a clear sky and a fine fresh breeze blowing up the fjord. Never have I had a more glorious sail. With sheets eased on a broad reach* Bowdoin *swept through the icy waters. . . . The arm of the fjord upon which the base was located was filled with slush ice. Bowdoin made an eerie sound as she swished through . . . until at last we dropped all sail and let her slide gracefully into her snug berth on the inner side of the pier.*[47]

Additionally, Greenland winds, known as the Foehn, are the result of a specific combination of temperature and atmosphere over the ice cap. Beneficial in that the temperature was warm, and any wind prevented much ice formation, so the survey work was not impeded; but difficult since the wind rose quickly to hurricane force. Hotchkiss described the first experience:

*The first gust of wind confirmed our worst expectations; it blew directly into the entrance of the harbor, converting the uninviting coastline into a lee shore. Quickly we got underway, in the desperate hope we could find protection elsewhere, but returned to the harbor. That evening the wind departed as quickly as it had come. During the storm, we had watched the barometer descend rapidly until the needle fetched up on the stop at the bottom of the scale. The next day it was still there. . . . When we hailed a Coast Guard trawler in the fjord, I asked for his barometer reading –27.67 inches. Our scale ended at 27.70! Eventually our barometer recovered.*[48]

*Bowdoin*'s second experience with the Foehn wind was at a berth at Julianehaab, alongside the rusty steamer *Tintagle,* with doubled lines and extra steel cables from the steamer, and all available fenders between them. The wind never dropped below 75 miles an hour, and the *Bowdoin* rolled constantly until her treenails started backing out. The men on seawatch reached over and reset them with a mallet.[49]

Later, Foehn winds were clocked at 165 miles an hour, but the schooner was safely berthed. The winds stopped at the end of March, and the *Bowdoin* was frozen in on the fjord for the month.

Hotchkiss learned he was to be replaced in the spring.[50] The *Bowdoin,* however, continued working in Greenland, under a new captain, John Backland. Naval officer John Backland from Seattle, who had been trading in Alaska during the summers on the four-masted schooner *C.S.Holmes,* took the *Bowdoin* north again to survey the inland passage from Narsarsusak to Ivigtut, Greenland. She sailed home uneventfully in early October 1943, down the Davis Strait. Aboard the *Bowdoin,* surveyor Joe Gorman made the voyage sound like a pleasure cruise:

> *We made a restful stopover at Sydney, Nova Scotia. Departing Sydney, we headed south through the freshwater Lakes of Bras d'Or. What a delightful passage that was: no heavy seas, and just the soft purr of the diesel engine as we all enjoyed a quiet night of rest. Finally, rounding Cape Sable, we met fair winds and a following sea and sailed along wing and wing for at ten knots for New England. Nearing the coast,* Bowdoin *ran into heavy fog.*

Fortunately, they sighted a fishing vessel dead ahead and followed it into the breakwater entrance of Gloucester.[51]

The USS *Bowdoin* was taken to Boston, where she was decommissioned and remained until the end of the war. MacMillan retired shortly before the war's end. Afterward, he received a telegram in January 1945, asking if he was interested in reclaiming the schooner, now listed as *Hulk #51.* She had been reduced to a derelict; everything of value aboard had been removed, and she was scheduled to be burned. [52]

However, MacMillan and Miriam reached her first at the Navy yard in Quincy, Massachusetts. They were distressed at her condition. MacMillan paid the Navy $4,000 for his schooner and gathered any parts that could be found in the shipyard, finding almost everything—except the engine.[53]

MacMillan supervised and shared in the workload necessary to repair the schooner, and others shared in his enthusiasm. MacMillan wanted a Cummins diesel engine, so the schooner was towed to the Cummins Diesel Company on the Charles River. When the 100-horsepower motor was installed, he received a receipt from the head of the company that read, "We have long been interested in your work, and hope you will continue it. Accept this engine as a gift."[54]

Repairs were quickly completed in the late spring of 1946, and MacMillan had time to make a month-long trip to Labrador. From the beginning, the *Bowdoin* was an exploratory vessel, MacMillan asserted. "I've been training 'Arctic experts' on the *Bowdoin*. I take college students along to serve as my crew. They pay a slight tuition, which helps defray the expenses of the trip, and in return get a liberal education in navigation and exploration." [55]

Sailing into uncharted waters could cause damage to the *Bowdoin*, but any area unknown to MacMillan aroused his interest. Furthermore, MacMillan knew she could be repaired in Maine.

From 1947 to 1953, MacMillan made five more trips in the *Bowdoin* north. L.L. Bean outfitted the crew, and MacMillan went supplied with ample film. Dr. Edward Morse joined the expedition as ship's physician in 1947, additionally training for dentistry to "help the communities they visited. MacMillan always wanted to offer aid, and medical expertise was needed. A doctor or pharmacist had been taken on earlier voyages."[56]

Morse was impressed with the geology and history of the north, where he could still see active glaciers at work. He recalled that sailing adventures were prevalent, and one day, well off the Greenland coast, they heard three thumps on the schooner's hull. There was nothing to see, though. The schooner "had struck a submerged ledge, [although] the fathometer showed plenty of water before and after. . . . MacMillan just marked it on the chart."[57] Another update duly noted, among many others.

When the *Bowdoin* reached 66 degrees 33 minutes north latitude, they celebrated by cheering, ringing the ship's bell, pumping the foghorn, and blowing the air whistle to commemorate crossing the Arctic Circle—only an imaginary line, but the *Bowdoin's* goal on each northern voyage.[58]

On this expedition, the *Bowdoin* went the farthest north—11 degrees latitude from the North Pole. The expedition conducted research for the U.S. Hydrographic Department, sounding fjords, correcting and updating charts—which now bore MacMillan's name—bringing supplies to the Nain school, documenting the wildlife; and, in 1949, bringing back "fossils which we gathered at the lower Savage Islands [that] are of the Cambrian Period of the Paleozoic Era and are, therefore, representative of the marine life of about 350,000,000 years ago. These are the oldest things we have brought back. . . . Man did not appear until 2,250,000 years later."[59]

In 1954, MacMillan set out on his last voyage with the *Bowdoin*. He sailed to Greenland and continued studies in botany, geology, ornithology, glaciology, as well as seamanship and navigation. Botanist Rutherford Platt, aboard for the 1946 and 1954 expeditions, later wrote: "With his schooner, that has never failed him, because he built her that way, Mac fills his life with far more adventure in a few weeks than other men could in a lifetime."[60]

The weather, which had "shown MacMillan about every side of itself in nearly a half century of sailing North, gave him enough special recognition this time. . . . The devil threw the book at us on this one."[61]

MacMillan, with a good ship under him, and a sound 100-horse-power engine, decided to sail, in spite of a brilliant red sky at dawn in Hopedale. Later that day, MacMillan noted in the log: "Raining and blowing from the Northeast. The barometer has fairly tumbled downhill and is now at 29.20." The *Bowdoin* raced along the coast under shortened sail, foresail and jumbo.

It was getting dark rapidly, and the seas were building up enough so that they began to tumble. The *Bowdoin* staggered in the cross-grained roll, racing on the crests, dropping into the troughs, and swinging her crosstrees through widening arcs. They had to find a harbor. MacMillan decided to run for Turnavik West, a hole between two islands.

The white water was closer; the blackness of the Labrador coast loomed to starboard. MacMillan was at the forward rigging, and the whole crew was topside in the event that they needed to abandon ship. He ordered, "Starboard a bit!" Then, "Hard starboard!" The *Bowdoin's* bow was headed directly for a roll of broken surf that filled the immediate horizon.

Abruptly the schooner slipped through a "rocky slot so narrow that the ledges on either side could have been touched with a boat hook." They were in a harbor so tiny that there wasn't room to put out an anchor. A small boat was launched, and the rock wall of the harbor was examined by flashlight for a ringbolt Mac-Millan remembered. He ordered, "Make our line fast to it." The *Bowdoin* was made fast by her bow and stern. MacMillan remembered the harbor from forty years earlier: "I saw a patch of black against the lighter sky. . . . Bob Bartlett's house. I just headed her straight for it."[62]

That night, Hurricane Hazel swept up the east coast of the United States and hit the Labrador coast with winds in excess of 100 miles an hour. Every fishing schooner in Ailik's Cove was sunk. Thanks to MacMillan's knowledge and his ability to remember the geography of places he had been, his schooner voyaged home unscathed.[63]

# 3

# Retirement

*It might have been different had there been several different vessels in his life, but the fact is that there was principally the* Bowdoin, *and in her, with her, he forged a life in which the two were, to a major degree, inseparable and indistinguishable.*
—BIOGRAPHER EVERETT S. ALLEN, 1962

FROM HIS VOYAGES ON THE *BOWDOIN,* MACMILLAN "WROTE SIX books (one is an unpublished manuscript), made numerous movies, updated countless charts, and compiled several dictionaries of the native Northern languages."[1] All the charts of North Labrador issued by the U.S. government now bore the name MacMillan, and much of what was once unnamed land now possessed definition and identity. He received many awards, and the president of the National Geographic Society, Dr. Gilbert Grosvenor, declared in 1927, "America and the world owe Commander MacMillan a debt of gratitude for the splendid contributions to knowledge of the Arctic he has made."[3]

Grosvenor presented MacMillan with the Hubbard Gold Medal in 1953, praising his work:

*For outstanding Arctic explorations from 1908 to 1952 and valuable service to geographic education and science. . . . MacMillan's achievements have been outstanding and continuous for forty-four years. I can find in history no explorer whose active devotion to solving the geographic secrets of the Arctic has continued for so long.*[4]

MacMillan's response to the Hubbard Gold Medal award was:

*All that work that I did, if it might be called work, was not in hopes of reward or honor. The fact that I was adding something, perhaps a tiny bit, to the sum total of human knowledge—that was my compensation, that was my reward.*[5]

MacMillan also received a second honorary Doctorate of Science degree in 1937 from Boston University.[6] Additionally, he was promoted to Rear Admiral in 1954.

*In recognition of your lifelong and invaluable services on the behalf of the United States and the U.S. Navy through outstanding contributions to the sciences of hydrography, meteorology, and geography in the polar areas.*[7]

Other recognitions included naming the Provincetown main road and town pier after him. On MacMillan's birthday at 80, Provincetown's nationally known poet, Harry Kemp, wrote a poem in his honor.[8] In 1967, the Peary MacMillan Museum opened at Bowdoin College, exhibiting MacMillan's history and work.[9]

"There are two great monuments to Mac: the museum and the *Bowdoin*," stated Miriam MacMillan.[10] However, his most tangible monument is his schooner.

His concern was the *Bowdoin*'s existence and condition after his retirement; he did not want to see this historic vessel, which had sailed over 200,000 miles in Northern exploration, sold to commercial interests or be abandoned. After his final voyage to the North in 1954, he began planning for her preservation. Perhaps the weather on his last voyage or his age of 84 influenced his decision, along with the advice of friends, to retire. Moreover, MacMillan believed he had found an appropriate home for the *Bowdoin*.

In 1959, she left on her nineteenth expedition with MacMillan, to the Mystic Seaport Museum in Mystic, Connecticut, to whom MacMillan had sold her for $4,000, first preparing her as if she were to embark on her next Arctic expedition. His compass and binnacle, wheel, chart table, bunks, and galley table remained on board the *Bowdoin*.[11] The museum was mounting an Arctic exhibit, and the *Bowdoin* was the ideal centerpiece.

A celebratory marine parade escorted the schooner to her berth at the pier, alongside the whaling ship *Charles W. Morgan* and the square rigger *Joseph Conrad*. Just before she docked, however, "the schooner demonstrated a certain individuality by nudging the bottom mud, and coming to a halt. Then, a little towboat took a line from the *Bowdoin*'s quarter, snaked her off in about three minutes, and the schooner went into her berth without incident by a newly cut channel.[12]

Connecticut's Lieutenant Governor Dempsey proclaimed June 27 as *Bowdoin* Day, and Phillip R. Mallory, president of the Marine Historical Association, stated that "Mystic Seaport is the work of hundreds of thousands who believe in the ideals we are trying to perpetuate today, and we all welcome with open hearts the schooner *Bowdoin*."[13]

MacMillan responded:

*I am thoroughly and humbly pleased at the honor which has been bestowed upon the* Bowdoin, *my men, Miriam and myself. We haven't lost her; we haven't lost the* Bowdoin. *We can come here any time we want and go aboard. She will have a good home here, for a hundred years or more.*[14]

This was MacMillan's hope. However, the museum's director, Eduoard Stackpole resigned, and the museum concentrated on upgrading its buildings instead of maintaining its exhibits. Those visiting her noticed the neglect. Nine years after MacMillan's presentation, *Bowdoin* was still afloat, but covered in plastic, and had begun to deteriorate.[15]

II

# On The Hard

## Restoration

4

# Refit

*The* Bowdoin *will sail again!*
—Donald Baxter MacMillan, 1968

Once again, the *Bowdoin* was rescued by those who knew her past and believed in her worth. MacMillan, now 93, became aware of her condition at the Mystic Seaport Museum, and offered her to anyone who would care for her. Mystic, however, did not want to release her to an individual.

So, in 1968, she was purchased for $1.00 from the Mystic Seaport Museum by the newly formed Schooner *Bowdoin* Association, headed by Dr. Edward Morse, and towed back to Maine.[1]

In the 1990s, Morse reflected on his Arctic experience on the *Bowdoin* voyage in 1947 and said, "You felt as if you were really getting to the frontier. The *Bowdoin* is a symbol, and it shaped my life."[2] Through his friendship with the MacMillans, he met his wife, Helga, who had been born at Jakobshavn, Greenland. For the next fifteen years, he was the president of the organization in charge of the schooner's guardianship.

The Schooner *Bowdoin* Association's planned restoration of the *Bowdoin* was begun by Captain Jim Sharp, who had purchased waterfront land to build a shipbuilding museum and needed an historic vessel to display on the pier. Sharp leased the schooner for $1.00 a year, paying for ten years in advance.[4]

Sharp began working on her after she was successfully towed to Camden. He replaced the mainmast with a 185-year-old Maine spruce, repaired the 25-year-old engine, and refinished much of the interior. In 1969, made sufficiently seaworthy, she sailed to Provincetown from October 5 to 26. Although the entire voyage was foggy, a clear sky temporarily appeared, and MacMillan came out on his porch and saw his schooner for the last time.[5] More than 300 people saw the schooner and gathered on the wharf to greet her.

MacMillan died at age 95 on September 10, 1970.[6] He is buried in the Provincetown cemetery, under a simple stone. The English poet Tennyson's lines for an earlier Arctic explorer are fitting:

> *. . . thou,*
> *Heroic sailor-soul,*
> *Art passing on thine happier voyage now*
> *Towards no earthly pole*
> —From "Sir John Franklin's Memorial,"
> Alfred, Lord Tennyson, 1877

Sharp returned to Camden and continued repairs. He worked with John Nugent, a former summer student who had sailed on the *Stephen Taber* and returned to Camden as an adult, working without pay at his own request on the *Bowdoin*. She became the Sharp family yacht, sailing along most of the eastern coast from the Chesapeake to Nova Scotia.[7]

Sharp also used the schooner as a work vessel, towing the engineless windjammers *Adventure* and *Stephen Taber* to and from their winter berths and retrieving water-soaked logs from the nearby islands.[8] For four years during the summer season she was also hired out for private charters skippered by Captain Alan Talbot.[9] Sharp rightfully claimed that a working vessel is maintained in better condition, and said, "If she'd been mine, I'd still be sailing her."[10] However, the work Sharp was subjecting the old schooner to was not in keeping with the educational plans the Schooner *Bowdoin* Association intended.

MacMillan had written in the foreword to the 1947 book *The Log of the Schooner* Bowdoin, by A. S. Horr:

> *There were to be no sailors in the crew! There have never been so-called sailors on the* Bowdoin *since the day she was launched in 1921, or during her more than one hundred thousand miles of Arctic work.*[3]

In 1975, Sharp and Orvil Young bought the schooner *Roseway*. The Schooner *Bowdoin* Association decided not to continue with Sharp's lease, and later that year, he was reimbursed the $4.00 that remained.[11] Sharp made the ambiguous statement: "I never did get rich from the *Bowdoin*. She was a piece of my soul at the time."[12] The dedicated John Nugent, however, stayed on to work.

Captain Carl Chase and Roger Brainard chartered the *Bowdoin* for the 1975 summer season of weeklong educational programs, as their windjammer, the *Nathaniel Bowditch*, was in financial difficulty.[13] Thus began the voyage back to education and exploration—for which the *Bowdoin* had been built. Carl's brother, Andy Chase, was the first mate at the time; he would later captain the *Bowdoin*.

On the *Bowdoin's* educational voyage to Isle au Haut, the mainmast Sharp had replaced broke at the crosstrees. The dismasting was caused by "a defect in the wood, there—you couldn't see it," explained Andy Chase. In a week, Billings Diesel in Stonington quickly fabricated a new mast from a steel pipe.[14]

From Carl Chase's programs, the Schooner *Bowdoin* Association later developed Inter-Island Expeditions in 1976, which continued to offer educational voyages.[15] John Nugent was the skipper—he was now certified as a captain and earlier had sailed as the master of the windjammer *Mistress*.[16]

The Weyerhauser Company donated a new mast, the *Bowdoin*'s fourth, in 1976, replacing the steel pipe Billings had made.[17] That year, Rudyard Kipling's book *Captains Courageous* was made into a TV movie, and for the film, the *Bowdoin* launched dories, having the only authentic ones for the time period, and was also in the background Camden harbor scenes. *Bowdoin*'s disappointed crew contended, "Although we were in period costumes, and filmed in several scenes, those were cut from the film."[18]

In 1979, the Schooner *Bowdoin* Association wanted to continue the educational programs, but the *Bowdoin* needed further work to meet Coast Guard requirements. The *Bowdoin* was towed up to the Goudy and Stevens Shipyard in East Boothbay, where MacMillan had maintained her, for the work. Later she was moved to Maine Maritime Museum, the site of the former Percy and Small Shipyard, since the Association could not afford to make a long-term financial commitment for a berth at Goudy's.[19]

At the museum, a group from Goudy's, including John Nugent, David Short, and other apprentices, continued work until 1981, when the Association could no longer fund the workers. John Nugent continued alone until 1983. Fund-raising for the *Bowdoin* began, and a grant from the National Trust for $95,000 in matching funds was awarded for the schooner's restoration.[20] For the next four years, several people worked to raise the necessary share.

Ginny Sides, an experienced fund-raiser for Wellesley College, had retired to Maine and worked along with Miriam MacMillan and Helga Morse, the wife of the Schooner *Bowdoin* Association's president, to raise the amount needed. "What keeps the fundraiser going is not the money, it's the spirit behind the gifts, the belief in something which the gifts represent," said Ginny. "It's fascinating to me how much the *Bowdoin* meant to so many people."[21]

However, in 1984, Dr. Morse decided to become the president emeritus of the Association. He was no longer the active president he had been for the past fifteen years; and shortly after, Ginny left. The decision was made to borrow the remainder of the matching funds. [22]

Bill Coughlin was an employee at *The Boston Globe* whose father was a master mariner. Being interested in the sea and history, he knew Leo Hynes, the owner of the windjammer *Adventure*. When Sharp purchased the *Adventure* from Hynes, Coughlin sailed in her, and wrote several articles about her for the newspaper.

At Sharp's suggestion, he met John Nugent on the *Bowdoin* in the fall of 1982. Seeing Nugent's dedicated solitary work on the project, Coughlin started driving from Boston up to Bath, Maine, to help, and others joined him.[23] Nugent continued his work until 1983 but was removed from his position by the Schooner *Bowdoin* Association, due to a change in leadership.[24]

Eventually she was fitted for a new marine engine and went down the ways again in October 1984. Miriam MacMillan was there, and MacMillan's niece May Fogg, now in her 70s, again threw flowers over her bow, as she had in 1921.[25] Through the efforts of George Collins of the *Boston Globe* Foundation, she was moved to the Charlestown Navy Shipyard in Boston, with a berth near the USS *Constitution*, where it was hoped she would attract more attention.[26]

Jim Sharp towed the *Bowdoin* from Camden to Boston on a cold January day in 1985.[27] That night, after being left at her berth, with secure lines and a working electric bilge pump set up with a plastic pipe discharging through a porthole onto the deck, the *Bowdoin* nearly sank in the heavy rain, sleet, and snow. The deck had filled with water, her scuppers had frozen, and without freeing ports due to her high bulwarks, water filled the boat. The automatic bilge pump kept dumping water onto the deck, and the water went below, due to the porthole being lower than the caprail.[28]

Bill Coughlin luckily checked on her that night, by "instinct." He found "she was well over her waterline." He climbed aboard and below saw that "the water was almost five feet deep throughout the schooner, and halfway up the side of the engine."[29] He could do nothing alone and called for help, remaining aboard all night and into the afternoon of the next day. Soon after, Coughlin, Nugent, and other longtime workers left the project.[30]

In May, the *Bowdoin* was towed to Rose's Marine in Gloucester to repair the work done by others while John Nugent was absent. Among the many parts donated and installed for the *Bowdoin's* restoration was a new 190-horsepower Cummins marine engine. This was given in exchange for the old engine, which the company thought was the oldest operational Cummins engine, as well as the first to be adapted for marine use, and they planned to place it in their museum.[31]

Individuals and corporations made, donated, and installed parts. Twin Disc donated and installed the gearbox and power take-off, as they had in 1946. Bath Iron Works designed, donated, and installed the exhaust system. For almost twenty years, more than 1,500 people worked, made, or donated parts or gave over $750,000 to restore the schooner.[32]

# Return

*I don't know if it's the design or her personality, but I could go
anywhere with her. I had the most fun docking her of any boat
I've ever known—I could make her spin around in circles—you
could try things you'd never even thinking of doing in another
boat. There was something about her that said, "It's OK."*

—Captain Bill Cowan

The *Bowdoin*'s next captain joined her while she was still
on the ways in Gloucester. Bill Cowan and his wife Jody moved
aboard her in May 1985, after delivering a cargo ketch across the
Pacific. Bill had been to the Arctic aboard the S/V *Regina Maris*
in 1982, and the *Bowdoin* was the most famous Arctic exploration
vessel known. He had enjoyed his year in the Arctic, "combining
sailing, sail training, scientific research, and northern exploration.
The *Bowdoin* epitomized this life . . . the *Bowdoin* was special."[1]
They quickly signed on with the famous old vessel.

Captain Cowan looked forward to helping complete a long list
of maintenance projects before she could return to Maine.[2] As the
executive director of the Schooner *Bowdoin* Association, Renny
Stackpole's first goal was to get the *Bowdoin* in sailing condition
and back to Maine.

After the work in Gloucester, a berth was found for the *Bow-doin* through contacts at *The Boston Globe* once again for six weeks at the Charlestown Navy Yard. Near the USS *Constitution*, there was more interest and assistance in finishing her. Working long hours, she was ready by early summer to return home.[3] After a reception at the Boston Yacht Club in Marblehead, the first of many fund-raising events, she readied for the voyage.[4]

Dr. Pete Rand, who had sailed with MacMillan in the 1950s, was the current president of the Schooner *Bowdoin* Association. He wrote of sighting her on the Fourth of July, 1985:

*After a sunny noontime of clan festivities on a seaside lawn in Cape Elizabeth . . . a glance out the window made me drop my fork. There she was, running in from the light buoy, wing and wing in a gentle southerly. Home again in Maine waters, the* Bowdoin *glided by Portland Head Light and into the harbor. The sight was a real heart-stopper.*[5]

Later, as the *Bowdoin* arrived in Penobscot Bay, the annual Great Schooner Race was ending; she joined the fleet of windjammers, who saluted her with their cannons, and she returned their greetings. Captain Cowan and the crew began finishing the schooner's systems and interior. Between the work, they sailed up and down the coast to fund-raisers.[6]

However, the Association needed more funds than could be raised, and Key Bank and National Sea Products assisted in the effort to certify the schooner according to the new Coast Guard Sail Training Vessel Standards.[7] Captain Cowan described the long and difficult process by the Coast Guard as thorough and careful, as well as respectful of the *Bowdoin's* historical integrity. She was successfully certified in 1986, the first certified sail training ship under America's National Sail Training Act.[8]

That spring the schooner took students out of Boston on a day sail, introducing them to seamanship and oceanography.[9] Once again, she had returned to her mission of exploration and education.

On June 22, 1986, the *Bowdoin* led the Op Sail parade on the Statue of Liberty's Centennial Celebration in New York Harbor. Unfortunately, *The Pride of Baltimore*, built in 1827, had just sunk in a microburst squall off the coast of Puerto Rico. The *Bowdoin* was asked to take the *Pride's* place. The schooner led the smaller Class B vessels, alongside the USCG S/V *Eagle*.[10]

The *Bowdoin* and the other Class B vessels gathered with the Class A vessels and more than 100 other boats. She was berthed at the South Street Seaport, rafted with SEA Education's *Westward*, which briefly caught fire but was extinguished without much damage. Lance Lee's Atlantic Challenge boats, *Egalite* and *Liberte*, from Rockport, Maine, were also nearby.[11]

Bobby Edwards, a contributor to the rebuild and a friend of Renny Stackpole, then the executive director of the Schooner *Bowdoin* Association, was aboard the *Bowdoin*. Eduoard Stackpole, Renny's father, had been the curator at Mystic when MacMillan installed the *Bowdoin* there; after he left, she had been neglected. She describes the parade:

> *Finally, the word came; the* Eagle *started out, we started out. I just can't tell you how exciting that was. . . . Down we went to the George Washington Bridge, and what was really exciting was that we went back down beside all the Tall Ships, and we could see each one coming in.*[12]

Later that year, the *Bowdoin* was docked beside the USS *Constitution*, as part of an Arctic history program at the city schools.[13]

Back in Maine, the Cowans were elated to continue with the schooner's life work of education.[14] A two-week archaeology course and sail training for secondary school students in Canada was the first program. Jody taught science, and Bill instructed in seamanship. This was a great success, although the weather was foggy for the entire voyage. Next was a research program in deep water with Bigelow Labs in Boothbay Harbor, in conjunction with Texas A&M University, measuring water temperatures and testing salinity.[15]

The Cowans affirm their support for the schooner:

*We worked very hard for the* Bowdoin *for very little, because it meant that much to us, and it still does. She was our whole life for two years, not a job. . . . We put our heart and soul into her . . .* [and] *We brought Miriam and Mac in spirit.*[16]

Next, the schooner was leased to the marine outdoor educational organization Outward Bound for eighteen months. She was back where she belonged, spearheading the next level of work for which she had been built and was now certified.

# III

# UNDERWAY

## In Maine Waters

## 6

# Outward Bound

*The boat will take you home.* Bowdoin *could handle anything;
she was accustomed to rough weather.*
— CAPTAIN CATE CRONIN, 2020

OUTWARD BOUND, THE TERM SIGNIFYING A VESSEL CLEARING
port to begin on a voyage, is ideal to describe all the *Bowdoin's*
endeavors. Moreover, it is appropriate that after meeting the new
Coast Guard regulations as the first United States Sail Training
ship, Passenger Vessel Ocean Sailing School Vessel, she returned to
marine education with this organization—the first outdoor education school, begun in 1942.[1]

This brief history highlights the ideals of the organization:

*Hurricane Island Outward Bound School was established in
1964 as the third Outward Bound school and only sea school
in this country. The concept of Outward Bound was begun by a
contemporary of MacMillan's, Kurt Hahn, who believed that the
foremost task of education was to insure survival of these qualities: an enterprising curiosity, an undefeatable spirit, tenacity in
pursuit, readiness, and above all, compassion.*

*The principal aim is to provide a format to teach those ideas, and the courses have all evolved from experience to use the wilderness, group participation, and self-discovery as tools toward those aims. Students at Outward Bound sites find themselves accomplishing things in areas that have largely been unfamiliar to them, such as rock climbing, sailing and navigating, and learning to operate closely with the natural environment as opposed to the urban experience. For one who might find the sailing experience exciting, but perhaps intimidating, Outward Bound crews are all novices when their voyages begin, proving that experience, under proper and compassionate leadership, is truly the best teacher.[2]*

Outward Bound encompasses the focus of the program's activities that train, support, and develop learners on the sea from all ages, abilities, and occupations. In Maine, the base for the sea program, participants in Hurricane Island Outward Bound School inhabit the coastal environment and become competent in survival techniques, living together first as a group, then alone for a few days in a solo component. Students learn to employ all the resources of the environment as well as those of each individual.

As with MacMillan's expeditions in the Arctic, the school provides a well-researched and carefully planned program, where students progress from eager neophytes to seasoned participants as they acquire new knowledge about themselves and their surroundings. Once again, the *Bowdoin* served as a stable platform from which to launch saltwater expeditions. Now at Maine Maritime Academy, Rick Miller, an Outward Bound instructor at the time, would later captain the schooner on her most recent voyage in 2008 back to the Arctic.

Cate Cronin began working in 1975 on the schooner *Adventure* as galley crew, and in various positions on other sailing vessels including the sloop *Clearwater*, schooners *Nathaniel Bowditch* and *Harvey Gamage*, and the brigantine *Westward*. After a few years as an Outward Bound instructor and working in educational programs and passenger trade in the Caribbean aboard the *Gamage*, she had gained sufficient sea time by 1978 to earn her 100-ton captain's license. Her license was more than these programs required, since her intention was only to be qualified to safely handle the pulling boats at Outward Bound.[3] Nonetheless, Captain Cronin was asked to skipper the *Clearwater*, whose captain was leaving. [4]

In 1980, she accepted the position as captain of the *Clearwater*, with its environmental education mission. Cate began with a seasoned crew, and as she was a new captain, their professionalism and the mentorship of *Clearwater's* former captain, Peter Wilcox, were assets. Captain Cronin was intrepid, sailing the 110-foot sloop in one of the most heavily used United States' waters near New York Harbor and on the Hudson River, and she earned respect from other captains.[5] Her ability to clearly communicate with all sorts of mariners was only one of her responsive characteristics. "Clearwater," a tug captain would call, "would you tell that sailboat near you that if they are not drawing thirty feet, then would they please get out of the middle of the channel?"[6]

However, Cate thought of herself as first an educator, not a sailor, and eventually left the *Clearwater* to go back to college, earning her masters in education from Harvard in 1985.[7]

The *Bowdoin* was inactive at the time, having recently undergone a significant restoration under the supervision of Captain John Nugent. The Schooner *Bowdoin* Association needed the support of an organization that could assume financial responsibility, reduce the substantial debt, and make the schooner self-sustaining.[8]

Due to Cate's educational experience, the *Bowdoin's* captain, Ken Shaw, contacted Cate. With others, they formed a plan.

When Cate began to organize the *Bowdoin's* programs, she first offered the schooner to Maine Maritime Academy, knowing that the academy may be able to use the *Bowdoin* in their programs as well as afford the upkeep needed. But President Ken Curtis declined the schooner; as he did not see what use she could serve at the academy.[9] Cate resumed her exhaustive search for support, appealing to programs, and the crew to implement the programs' needs. Eventually, she agreed to host a variety of educational programs as captain and program director on the *Bowdoin*.[10]

A brochure for the programs Cate offered included this description:

> *Hurricane Island Outward Bound School Aboard a Living Legend: The Schooner* Bowdoin. *An experience that combines the adventure of sail with an opportunity for personal growth and self-discovery through hands-on sail training, group participation, and environmental awareness, located from the Chesapeake Bay to the coast of Maine.*
>
> *Hurricane Island Outward Bound recently acquired the use of the historic schooner* Bowdoin *for a new series of sea-based programs. The current role of this vessel continues its legacy of exploration, learning and self-discovery that has been its hallmark since its launching in 1921. The man who commissioned the* Bowdoin, *though a scientist by profession, recognized the opportunity for personal growth and learning that a sailing vessel provided. Even before taking groups of students to the Arctic, he taught sailing and outdoor skills to youths at his summer camp on the coast of Maine....*

*The students who worked as crew aboard the* Bowdoin *on the eighteen trips with MacMillan to the Arctic and northern coastal regions had, in fact, something of the Outward Bound experience in learning to cope with an exciting but often dangerous and unforgiving environment. MacMillan saw the need of developing "the whole person—spirit, mind, and body" and was also interested in providing a closer contact and appreciation of the natural environment.*[11]

The remarkable setting supplied by the schooner is a safe and seaworthy base.

*The schooner was built by William Hand, recognized for his practical interpretations of Gloucester fishing schooners. Now in her 65th year of service, she has proven her seaworthiness beyond question, not unlike the Outward Bound pulling boats designed by contemporary naval architect Cyrus Hamlin, modeled after the lifesaving surfboats of the early nineteenth century. She has exceptional blue-water stability but is also adaptable for visits to coastal rivers and bays, and carries modern electronics, diesel power and meets all Coast Guard Sailing School requirements.*

*All programs are built around challenging activities. . . . The operation of a schooner depends upon the same development of skills and teamwork. . . . This schooner program can be accomplished with a variety of groups, and in different geographic areas.*[12]

Cate's knowledge and relationship with the *Bowdoin* began in 1978.

*I was an assistant watch officer with HIOBS sailing across Penobscot Bay with a dozen teenagers on a month-long Outward*

*Bound course when I saw the familiar rig of the* Bowdoin. *We sailed alongside so I could see if Captain Jim Sharp might be aboard—since having worked for Jim, a few years earlier, I knew he sometimes sailed the* Bowdoin *to Eagle Island.*

*Instead of finding Captain Sharp, it was Captain John Nugent aboard, with the help of University of Maine graduate student Wes Hedlund. Wes was leading the marine science component for one of the Infinite Odyssey sailing and island adventure programs for Boston inner city youth. My crew of students aboard our 30 foot pulling boat and Wes' students were impressed by the "small world" nature of coastal Maine, when it became clear that Wes and I knew each other from Bangor High School; Wes had taught science there when I was a student.*

*Such a coincidence of seeing each other out on the bay warranted an offer for me come aboard for a day when my course was over. I always said yes to an invitation to get a sail on any vessels in those years and was accumulating skills and knowledge about the ways in which boats can be a platform for enriching experiences. Although I was close to getting my Coast Guard license and knew I would continue to seek work with educational programs, I couldn't have foreseen then that my first sail aboard the* Bowdoin *might lead to establishing new opportunities for both me and the schooner.*[13]

A decade later, Cate was leading the *Bowdoin*'s programs for HIOBS, and discovered that

*the best asset for this new Schooner* Bowdoin *Program was the versatility and safety of the schooner for sail training, self-discovery, and team building programs. To create experiential and team building programs for adults or teens, educators and executives, near shore and offshore, the essential requirement is to operate the boat safely, while ensuring a high level of participation. The schooner* Bowdoin *allowed both of these with its size and flexibility in use of sail and power.*[14]

Cate offers an example of when she and her crew were

*using the schooner creatively for different types of experiences. In Boston Harbor we provided a one-day experiential team building program for educational leaders enrolled in the Harvard Graduate School of Education. We knew this group would want to be challenged and we only had a few hours to provide the most effective team building we could.*

*After greeting the twenty plus participants and providing safety guidelines while motoring away from the dock and commercial traffic lanes, we invited them to organize themselves into a crew and get the schooner under sail within half an hour. When they were still talking through their strategy and seeking who might have any sailing knowledge after twenty minutes or so, we felt they needed a sense of urgency to take action, so I cut the engine, and said the crew will let them know if they are making serious or dangerous errors, and it was up to them to get the boat sailing. This added a sense of urgency, which can happen in real situations, and added to the rich debrief conversation about their learning from this hands-on teamwork experience.*

*The simplicity and ease of setting sail made this team initiative an excellent program element which we used again for youth courses as well. Outward Bound instructors have used the surprise element of asking students to figure out how to get the 30-foot pulling boats underway before any training was offered. Using the same initiative, but on a vessel three times the size, was unexpected, and what made the schooner* Bowdoin *a valued part of the school's fleet.*

*The* Bowdoin *is under the command of a highly qualified Coast Guard licensed captain, qualified instructors, with students forming the crew, learning new skills and disciplines while underway. This is a natural learning experience, as there is something about a schooner that invites participation. Students aboard the* Bowdoin *will learn 'the ropes' of responsibility, seamanship, navigation, sail theory, ship's maintenance and food preparation as well as an opportunity for personal growth and development, caring for each other with a better appreciation and concern for the environment. Students range in age from fourteen years to their seventies.*[15]

*The courses are styled after those ashore, using the boat as a challenge site, i.e. climbing rigging safely as a confidence builder, plotting courses, and handling unexpected weather. Ship's routine will be part of daily life along with learning maritime history, local environmental awareness, social interaction and some reflective time alone. The keeping of a journal (or personal log) is a good way to record feelings and events throughout the course.*

*The Hurricane Island Outward Bound experience aboard the historic schooner* Bowdoin *is one that can grow by reflection long after you have come ashore. Being a part of a tangible legacy of the age of sail, gaining a different perspective on your environment and learning to operate in a small community that is interdependent by the necessity of safely and successfully operating a sailing vessel are just some of the opportunities for personal growth.*[16]

All the available seagoing Outward Bound courses on the schooner will advance

*One of the most important aspects of a school, organization or corporation is the development of focused goals, teamwork and communication. This is dependent on good interaction between leaders and group members. Though there is often insufficient time available, Outward Bound has successfully run programs that bring people together under conditions that promote understanding and self-development, and now expands that concept to special group contract courses aboard the* Bowdoin.

*The courses provide opportunity to bring together students and faculty, principals and teachers, youth groups, community groups and management teams. This is effective since while on board, all group participants are working towards the same initiatives and learn interaction in a setting outside the formal organizational structure. This is achieved through hands on running of the schooner, challenging physical and self-discovery activities, and group dependence in an "outdoor classroom."* [17]

Furthermore, an excellent training use of the *Bowdoin*'s usual

*east coast transits each spring and fall from Maine to Norfolk, Virginia, as the schooner wintered over at the Chesapeake Maritime Museum in St. Michaels, Maryland, was to bring Outward Bound staff aboard for informal sailing and as extra crew. We had done this between the Chesapeake Bay and New York City in the spring of 1988, and after our New York based programs were done, we invited the New York Outward Bound staff for the leg to Boston's Thompson Island. Unfortunately, after our guest crew departed in Boston, we still planned an additional trip to make a visit to Admiral MacMillan's home in Provincetown.*

*In thick fog, and with fewer than the ideal number of crew members, we managed the trip to meet some of the local residents.*

*The Provincetown Museum had put the word out to come see the schooner and we didn't want to cancel, so with our newly donated radar, we came out of the fog to hear a few hearty folks welcome us with applause, delighted to see the schooner again.*

*We didn't stay long, as we needed to get back to Boston. With building seas and northerly winds, we determined that a reach across Massachusetts Bay to Duxbury was far better than beating to windward or motoring into the winds. With only three of us as deck crew, we were relieved to tuck into Duxbury's harbor and wait it out. We were glad to have made the Provincetown trip on this voyage north and still make it to Boston for our next spring programs.*[18]

With all the work on the *Bowdoin*, Cate was building the future that MacMillan had initiated decades ago: teaching seamanship and sailing while exploring with students. If the *Bowdoin* were to have a healthy future, what could be more appropriate than education?[19]

"It took one hundred percent—no, a thousand percent of my energy," claimed Cate.[20] Nevertheless, she was able to demonstrate that the schooner could meet the triple accomplishments of being self-supporting, meeting the requirements of education, and remaining in good condition.[21]

Although Outward Bound did not renew their lease with the *Bowdoin*, preferring to concentrate on their original programs, she had been established as a reliable platform for a broad range of educational activities, and attracted attention as a functioning historic vessel. After being proven, when Cate again offered her to Maine Maritime Academy, the outcome was different.

Through Cate's expertise, the *Bowdoin* was safely brought intact into the latter part of the twentieth century.

# 7

# Maine Maritime Academy

*It was incredible to see her actually pull it off. This boat will sail into anything.*

—CAPTAIN ANDY CHASE, 1989

THE *BOWDOIN* FOUND A NEW HOME AT MAINE MARITIME ACADemy and came into the Academy's Castine dock on the Friday after Thanksgiving, 1988.[1] "The day was frigid, and it was blowing hard—a *Bowdoin* breeze,"[2] said Captain Cronin.

Captain Andy Chase was now her skipper, the *Bowdoin*'s former first mate from thirteen years earlier, when his brother had leased the schooner for weekly educational programs, initiating her return to her original purpose. Captain Cronin and others from Outward Bound joined a crew from the academy and sailed her from Rockland to Castine.[3]

That weekend, the crew prepared the schooner for the winter; she was put to bed by Sunday afternoon.[4] Symbolic of the new institution that would provide her care, the schooner had come to Maine Maritime through a student's concern, aware that the *Bowdoin* was seeking a permanent home. Midshipman Chris Kluck had contacted Andy Chase with the idea that the *Bowdoin* would be helpful to the Academy for the sail training program and for public relations.[5]

Maine Maritime Academy President Ken Curtis accepted the Schooner *Bowdoin* Association's lease to the academy with option to buy. He had become aware of the vessel's importance through Chris Kluck's petition and while sailing in the schooner *William Albury* in Miami, Florida—noting how much attention the vessel drew. The fee was to make the loan payments, and the price was to assume the debt she carried. After the sale of a large sailing yacht given to the academy, the *Bowdoin* was home.[6]

In the spring of 1989, Chase and First Mate Elliot Rappaport and crew thoroughly cleaned and refurbished the schooner. A Marine Advisory Board was established to supervise her use. Among others, John Nugent and Bill Cowan were appointed to the board. The *Bowdoin* sailed along the coast of Maine on a capital campaign for the academy, as she had with Captain Cowan in 1985.

Increasingly, the schooner began to fulfill an associated instructional position in addition to her traditional mission of Arctic exploration. When purchased, the *Bowdoin* was intended to "serve a multi-faceted mission, acting as a sailing ambassador for the Academy, while enabling the college to include sail training in its expanding curriculum of nautical science and ocean studies."[7]

Furthermore, *Bowdoin*'s role has steadily expanded at the Academy. After an initial season spent making capital campaign appearances, she was returned, under the MMA banner, to the role for which she was conceived: education and exploration of the Arctic.

During 1989, Captain Chase, who had been assigned to skipper the schooner, was sailing the *Bowdoin* in nearby waters and "developing routines, trust and understanding and expectations of her, and seeing what changes needed to be made before undertaking more significant voyages."[8] He was also responsible for the crew's seamanship training, with extensive instruction and practice in navigation.[9]

Chase describes her entrance to Boothbay Harbor that year:

*Once again,* Bowdoin *impressed us with her willingness to tack in virtually no wind, with only a half–dozen boat lengths to get way on between tacks. Her headway was all but imperceptible, yet she never failed to tack, and the result was we were able to work our way dead to windward up a crowded and narrow harbor under sail.*[10]

And in the islands of Penobscot Bay:

*By late afternoon we had a light southerly breeze, and a fair tide once again, so we sailed in beside Brimstone and the east shore of Vinalhaven to Winter Harbor. . . . We just kept poking in further and further under sail, so we had come far enough so we couldn't bear to turn on the engine. In the end, we managed to beat up a channel that was at its narrowest just three-and-a-half boat-lengths wide. It was incredible to see her actually pull it off. This boat will sail into anything.*[11]

Farther along:

*We managed to squeak, squeeze, and wriggle our way all the way up to the head of Seal Bay, to drop the hook under Hay Island, in what must be the most protected anchorage in the world.*[12]

The high point of the summer was a trip to Halifax on July 25. They encountered a variety of typical north coastal weather, mostly the well-known fog. An uncomfortable incident on that day at 5:00 p.m., however, occurred with a

*most peculiar wind fluke . . . it must have been a mini-micro-burst. We were sailing along with about 10-15 knots from the southwest on a reach when out of nowhere, she jibed. A puff had sprung up from the northwest—just one puff. Then it went calm. Then she jibed back—a new puff from the southwest. Within a minute or two we were back underway as before, but we were all a little nervous. I stayed that way all night.*[13]

Such a wind burst had sunk the *Pride of Baltimore* only three years before, as Chase knew.

Nevertheless, they used dead reckoning and soundings to plot their way and arrived only a mile and a half off course, without the Loran. Halifax Traffic was surprised, informing them that they were east of the harbor channel. Her captain explained that "I needed the sea room to jibe over to fetch the next run."

They responded: "Oh, I see *Bowdoin*, we didn't realize you were under sail."

"They must've figured us for crazies—storming in through a thick-o-fog under full sail," Chase realized.[14]

He described the return voyage, with more fog:

*We made a smuggler's entrance into Bar Harbor at 0200 this morning—in a dungeon fog and pitch dark. Visibility was somewhat less than zero, but the bay is a good one for that kind of run. We passed Egg Rock Light (a 13-mile light), less than 4/10s of a mile off, and never even saw a glow. We groped our way right up into the harbor and dropped the hook just outside the line of anchored boats and hit the sack. In the morning, I headed back out to sea—to get outside the traffic and the rocks, and also to try to get back the rhythm of the voyage. I wasn't ready to give up the trip just yet.*[15]

Moreover, right here at home in Maine they faced some of the navigational difficulties the *Bowdoin* had seen in the North with MacMillan, Chase wrote. For example, at Machais Seal Island he found "unmarked shoals there, and swift currents, not to mention a local magnetic disturbance."[16]

Furthermore, despite Chase's painstaking attention, the schooner continued her customary habit of innocuous collisions with assorted marine obstructions on her voyages.[17] He explained the first grounding in Atkins Bay in mid-June:

*It makes a good anchorage, if you don't get past the range formed by the old state pier remains—which I did. I was just rounding up when* Bowdoin *took a very gentle heel to port and stopped. We were well parked, and only gently, with an incoming tide, so we held a grounding drill. The kedge anchor (a 75-pound Danforth) was got into the boat with two dock lines bent on and run out to windward. Taking to the windlass, we were able to heave her bow into the wind slowly, and in twenty minutes we were afloat again.*[17]

In 1989, pleased with the *Bowdoin*'s performance, Captain Chase asserted: "She's a fabulous boat, as good a boat as you can get."[18] That year, the *Bowdoin* was registered as a United States Historic Landmark, as if to echo his appreciation. The year before, the schooner had been adopted by the State of Maine as the official state vessel. Nominated by the academy's administration, the college's in-state location reinforced her connection, and she was so designated by the governor and the legislature on August 4, 1988.

James P. Delagado, a well-known maritime historian at the National Park Service completed the *Bowdoin*'s registration form of the National Register of Historic Places on June 30, 1989. He described the *Bowdoin* accurately from MacMillan's plans and cited her historic importance.[19]

More public relations visits were made all along the Maine coast for the rest of the summer, raising $1,000,000 for the academy. The schooner's contribution was applauded, and the *Bowdoin* was prepared for the winter.[20]

Maine Maritime Academy student Charlie Orn slushes the rigging as the students prepare the schooner *Bowdoin* for a trip to the Arctic in Castine on May 14, 2008. Slushing the rigging keeps the wire from corroding and rusting. (Photo by Tim Greenway/*Portland Press Herald* via Getty Images)

Schooner *Bowdoin* second mate Christopher Moore drills a hole in the main boom as Captain Richard Miller looks on. (Photo by Tim Greenway/*Portland Press Herald* via Getty Images)

Maine Maritime Academy students prepare the schooner *Bowdoin* for a trip to the Arctic in Castine on May 14, 2008. (Photo by Tim Greenway/*Portland Press Herald* via Getty Images)

Hila Shooter, at left, from Monroe, Maine, waves to a friend as she helps dock the schooner *Bowdoin*. Shooter, a student at the Maine Maritime Academy, was on the schooner with Arctic youth ambassadors. The boat came into Portland in May 2008 right before an international forum on the Arctic, the first one in the United States outside of Alaska. (Photo by Brianna Soukup/*Portland Press Herald* via Getty Images)

Arctic youth ambassadors pose for a photo onboard the schooner *Bowdoin* after docking in Portland. (Photo by Brianna Soukup/*Portland Press Herald* via Getty Images)

Donald B. MacMillan, 71, is seen at the wheel of the *Bowdoin* preparing for its 25th voyage north. (Photo by *Toronto Star* Archives/*Toronto Star* via Getty Images)

June 1939, Boothbay Harbor, Maine. Chauncey Waldron, who will supervise the iceberg study on MacMillan's 18th expedition to the Arctic aboard the schooner *Bowdoin*, is shown demonstrating to the crew how he and MacMillan will check the glacier movements with a theodolite. (Photo by Bettman via Getty Images)

MacMillan inspects the engine. (Photo courtesy Captain Will McLean)

The *Bowdoin* faces rough seas in the Laurentian Channel. (Photo courtesy Captain Will McLean)

*Bowdoin* sailing off the coast of Maine. (Photo courtesy Captain Will McLean)

*Bowdoin* out for repairs. (Photo courtesy Captain Will McLean)

Captain McLean polishes brass while underway. (Photo courtesy Captain Will McLean)

Captain McLean gives a lesson on points of sail and maneuvers under sail.
(Photo courtesy Captain Will McLean)

Heading out to sea. (Photo courtesy Captain Will McLean)

Ready for launch. (Photo courtesy Captain Will McLean)

The *Bowdoin* under power in Boothbay Harbor. (Herb Douglas photo)

# Returning to the Arctic

*It built to Force 8 or 9, and the seas were 15 to 20 feet and breaking. The boat took it elegantly.*

—Captain Andy Chase, 1991

Maine Maritime Academy President Ken Curtis and Captain Andy Chase knew the importance of taking the *Bowdoin* back to the Arctic. Geology professor William Powers, on the 1946–1954 expeditions, had written to MacMillan: "Going north with you and Miriam, in the *Bowdoin*, was the high point among all the things that I had ever done."[1] More responses such as these were an affirmation of the schooner.

The schooner's voyage to Nova Scotia in 1989 had been a preparatory voyage, as well as an opportunity for Chase to go north for the first time. After reading MacMillan's books, he realized MacMillan had sailed only ten days to reach the Labrador coast, so he decided to return with the *Bowdoin* for the first time to Nain, Labrador, in 1990.[2]

First, however, the schooner needed a new galley. First Mate Elliot Rappaport, along with John Steer, who had just graduated from the academy's Yacht Design Department, spent the winter of 1989 renovating the schooner's galley, installing a new refrigerator/

freezer. When replacing the steward's berth after the renovation, they added other berths.[3]

At noon on Sunday, July 1, the *Bowdoin* left Castine. Chris Kluck was aboard as the second mate and engineer with Captain Andy Chase, and the first mate, Elliot Rappaport, along with nine students, eight from Maine Maritime Academy. Two berths were available for paying visitors, and for five weeks Steve Kloehn, a reporter from *The Bangor Daily News,* and Tom Stewart, a photographer, among others, joined the crew.[4]

Chase describes the first taste of Northern weather as the schooner left Red Bay, Labrador, in the Strait of Belle Isle:

*We left Red Bay about 1600 in a veritable gale. It was a Kabbatic wind off the mountain—just as warm as could be and blowing about 30. We steamed up into the Basin and set sail (full main) and came out past the wharf doing about 8 knots. Hardening up, we set out through the channel and got a gust that buried our rail completely. It was quite a thrill for all, and the first real test of the rig. The minute we cleared the harbor entrance, in the span of a few seconds, the temperature dropped about 40 degrees.*[5]

Due to his inexperience with the northern coast, Chase had arranged for a pilot who could guide them, planning to stay offshore. "But coming in to Nain from the sea would probably be more difficult than staying inside all the way up. And by the time I had gotten to Labrador, I'd gotten a little more brazen," he commented.[6] So, the schooner continued her traditional route along the coast.

Chase was as demanding as MacMillan had been, although MacMillan was training scientists to be crew members as well as young students. Safety training, man-overboard drills, and seamanship exercises began immediately. The crew was organized into a flexible Swedish watch, and classes began.[7]

By July 17, the sunset was at 2200, and darkness began around midnight. "It never did get completely dark," observed Chase, and "By 0400 it was light enough to come back up to full speed."[8] In 1990, the *Bowdoin* carried all the modern navigation equipment, including a weather fax with surface and atmospheric weather maps, Canadian ice maps updated twice a day, as well as a radio-link medical call service. However, the Labrador landscape was as erratic and unmarked as in MacMillan's day.

"There are two buoys on the chart that covers about 1,000 square miles—there is one can and one nun inside Hopedale Harbor. There are also two whole lighthouses," Chase described the sparse navigational aids.[9] "While the next chart covered only 875 square miles, it had only a single lighthouse and lacked any buoys. There was a path marked with soundings through the middle of the chart." On the first Labrador voyage, heading for Nain under sail, the charting was quite accurate; much of the research for the map had been done on the *Bowdoin* by MacMillan.[10]

Photographers from *The National Geographic* and a film crew from the Canadian Broadcast Company in a speedboat came out to meet the *Bowdoin* as she entered Nain Harbor, where a crowd was on the dock waiting to view the schooner's mastheads coming around the point, just as they had in MacMillan's day.[11] Chase describes the schooner's dramatic entry:

> *We bore off and ran wing and wing straight toward the public dock where a crowd was indeed gathered in the cold and damp. Showing off, we ran straight up to the dock, jibed over about a boatlength off the dock and rounded up, striking sail as we rounded to. I let go a cannon blast as we swung past them. We were flying*

*the big maroon* Bowdoin *pennant at the masthead, the MMA flag at the main crosstrees, and at the fore crosstrees we flew a string with the Canadian flag at the top, the provincial flag of Newfoundland and Labrador in the middle, and the Labrador flag at the bottom with its blue, white and green, with a green spruce sprig. The U.S. ensign flew from the peak of the main gaff.*[12]

Everyone enjoyed the show, and when the *Bowdoin* left that Sunday, July 22, a crowd again gathered to see the schooner embark. The sail was raised at the dock, and they gave a cannon salute as they left. They visited Hopedale, and slipped into West Turnavik, where the *Bowdoin* had taken shelter from Hurricane Hazel in 1954. An acquaintance of the captain—Tony Williamson, a professor at Memorial University, St. Johns, Newfoundland—joined the crew and discussed the historic and current events of the coast they were passing.[13]

An experiment with the ice anchor was less successful, and although they moored the schooner in a little harbor on a beautiful iceberg about 80 feet tall, Chase was not comfortable with staying there longer than necessary.[14] At St. Johns, Williamson left, and the *Bowdoin* met the S/V *Corwith Cramer*, one of the three brigantines from the SEA Education Association in Woods Hole, Massachusetts. Chase had captained the *Westward* for them and acknowledged that "they were a fine sight, bearing down with everything flying."[15]

Going home, the crew sailed along with tape over the GPS, obliging the students to practice navigation by dead reckoning (DR), and the fathometer, as well as the occasional sun line. The schooner finished outside Halifax, off about 2 miles south—"Not bad for four days on DR," Chase conceded.[16]

He began to consider next year's schedule, confirming another voyage north when MMA President Curtis greeted him on his return with: "This is wonderful; you've got to go north again."[17] The decision was made to avoid the ice around Baffin Island in 1991. Instead, Chase planned to bring the schooner to Disko Island off Greenland, then return across Davis Strait by way of Cape Chidley and Bowdoin Harbor, then down to Labrador, Newfoundland, and Nova Scotia.

In 1991, on June 30, the *Bowdoin* left Castine bound for Greenland. A month and 2,000 miles later, the schooner crossed the Arctic Circle and was finally sailing among icebergs in the waters for which she was designed. On this voyage, she eventually sailed 150 miles north of the Arctic Circle.[18]

With Captain Andy Chase, First Mate Elliot Rappaport, Second Mate Zachary Thomas, Chris Kluck as second engineer, and Deborah Harrison as steward were nine Maine Maritime Academy students. Two berths were available for guests, as before. And, as before, Steve Kloehn, a *Bangor Daily News* reporter, and photographer Tom Stewart accompanied the crew for five weeks. Toward the end of the voyage, one especially welcome visitor was Captain Stuart Hotchkiss, who had last been aboard in 1943.[19]

Aboard the *Bowdoin,* as on the previous year's voyage, a Swedish watch was established, with day watches of six hours, and night watches of four hours; allowing twelve hours off every third day. Although the time was partially occupied with classes, the crew had many opportunities to enjoy the distinctive qualities of the voyage.

As in 1990, Chase began seamanship classes immediately; emergency drills made up the first lessons, then the specifics of the gear and the *Bowdoin's* rig. Reefing the main, setting and tacking the trysail, maneuvering sails to include the concept of balance under sail were taught and practiced.[20] On the schooner, classes took place "on the deck in nice weather, below deck when it was rotten, and cancelled when it was really rotten."[21]

As in the year before, course offerings included meteorology, seamanship, magnetic variation, anchoring, Arctic whaling, identifying whales and whale populations, Arctic culture, and, unexpectedly, provisioning. MacMillan had earlier written that if he had two years' supply of flour and coal—with hunting the native species, heat, and bread—he could survive.[22] Deborah had much more leeway and variety, but had to ration the "most important supply of chocolate;"[23] and she included fifty pounds of salt, so in an emergency she could salt down the meat and not lose it if the freezer failed.[24]

As they left Nova Scotia and sailed along the coast, the *Bowdoin*'s deck offered displays of the Northern lights in the evenings and whale and dolphin sightings in the mornings, with the first ice seen July 7 near Newfoundland.[25]

When the schooner encountered pack ice in a low concentration of floes, the captain decided to touch one. He bumped a piece, "just to see what we were up against. It just went mush."[26] However, Greenland's glacier ice floats westward until it is released into the North Atlantic, threatening ship traffic before eventually melting.

Continuing along up the northeastern Newfoundland coast, the *Bowdoin* sailed out into the Labrador Sea, and on July 22 saw a Greenland mountain on the radar, 60 miles away.[27] Three days later they landed at Godthaab, went on to Manitsoq, and made a detour to a "summer ski area," led by a local fisherman as a guide.

On the way back from the "jaunt," which began with a 12-mile sail, then a 7-mile hike and an overnight in a ski camp, it began to rain. Additionally, it was low tide, and the wind was blowing hard, directly at them. The captain later wrote:

*We were going out through a tricky place for which there was no chart, with a pilot who spoke not one word of English, into a Greenland Gale. [But,] Jens knew his route—we never saw less than three meters under our keel—and soon we were back on the chart, leaping into a mean, steep eight-foot sea. When we rounded the corner and were briefly abeam to it we took a couple of death rolls, and shipped the first green sea aboard. Jens was very impressed with the boat; he said several times: 'good boat, good boat.'*[28]

Their skillful guide knew two words of English, after all.

The *Bowdoin* finally crossed the Arctic Circle, at 66 degrees 33 minutes latitude, on July 28, 1991, for the first time in more than 35 years. A ritual for the first-time crossers was enacted, but, Chase noted,

*All the while, the barometer was dropping. . . . The northerlies kept building, and by midnight it was really blowing, cold and raining. It built to Force 8 or 9, and the seas were 15 to 20 feet and breaking. The boat took it elegantly. She was practically comfortable, except in the foc's'le, where she gave quite an elevator ride. We only rarely got swept by a sea. . . . Just once she punched into one and took a good deal of green water aboard. It was incredible to see her take it with such ease. And the crew held up perfectly.*[29]

When the wind dropped late the next morning, coming from the west, they found they had been blown about a dozen miles back across the 70th parallel. They returned to 70 degrees 1 minute north, and the *Bowdoin* rested inside a headland known as Akunaq Point, which was defined in the schooner's copy of MacMillan's 1938 dictionary quite appropriately as "the midpoint of one's journey."[30]

Crew members took the Zodiac ashore to build a cairn to mark the voyage's northernmost point. Captain Chase wrote, "The twilight was gentle, not vibrant—and remained fully bright enough to read and write on deck until sunrise came at 0130."[31] Heading back south, they returned to Disko Bay and Jakobshavn, Greenland.

The local glacier there creates 70 percent of the icebergs in the North Atlantic, although it takes two years for them to float into the North Atlantic traffic lanes. The glacier is 5 miles wide and a half-mile thick, advancing 75 feet each day. Every two days, it breaks off enough ice to supply all of New York City for a week. A bar at the mouth of the fjord holds the ice chunks until an abnormally high tide releases as many as a thousand bergs over a couple hours into the bay.[32] Two Danish Navy patrol vessels are stationed there, and on one a retired master was compiling a Greenlandic Coast Pilot Guide for Denmark. He stated that north of the Arctic Circle, charts are accurate for distances, soundings, and ranges, but latitude and longitude are only roughly calculated. Sailors have the same experience as MacMillan had taking star sights in 1921. Even GPS places them theoretically on land while factually afloat.[33]

Additionally, due to lack of darkness, Elliot wrote that

*the body doesn't know when to sleep. Every single day was more incredible than the one before, and you didn't want to sleep, you might miss something. Then your body would be feeling strange, and you'd realize you hadn't slept in 36 hours.*[34]

The *Bowdoin* crossed Davis Strait westerly, sailed past the remoteness of the Northern Labrador coast, and on to Port Burwell, Cape Chidley, and Bowdoin Harbor, which proved uninviting. Nevertheless, the schooner entered the namesake harbor, where Elliot explained,

*We had to strike sail and claw upwind to reach Bowdoin Harbor. To poke your nose into the 100-yard wide entrance on a day like*

*this one leaves you totally committed, and to lose power would mean going ashore. Bowdoin Harbor was a disappointment, at least for protection. In the eastern end, the wind sets down in blasts that blow craters in the water as if they were mortar rounds. The gale still blew fiercely in the morning. A group went ashore. . . . They reported that it was quiet outside, although the deep and narrow configuration of the valley, combined with the wind direction made for vicious winds just within the harbor. The* Bowdoin's *anchors came up from what may have been the windiest point on the whole coast.*[35]

Around 6:00 p.m., the lookout called everyone on deck. On the westward edge of the anchorage, a single polar bear stood, sniffing. Moving downwind and catching their scent, he ambled away after watching for a while.[36]

After supper, six crew went ashore to see a cairn built in 1934. Elliot wrote:

*The cairn sat undisturbed on the hilltop, covered with moss and with a tiny patch of tundra clinging to the rock in its lee. The presence of man represented in such a diminutive a fashion against this landscape seemed to heighten the desolation. Far below, the* Bowdoin *swung at anchor, a ghost returned.*[37]

The gale still blew in the morning, and the *Bowdoin* weighed anchor and proceeded out of Bowdoin Harbor into several days of

*the most difficult navigation Chase has ever experienced. To pilot a vessel on this coast is a meticulous and totally unrelenting task, with tenuous trails of soundings strung out across the white abysses of chart paper like invisible stepping-stones. The fathometer goes tic-tic-tic, your toes remain curled and your muscles tensed for the seemingly inevitable crunch of boat on stone. There is never a break to be afforded by putting yourself in the clear, and few places to get out of this . . . even if you had to. Notations make only nominal sense. An illustriously named "island" might be merely an oversize breaking ledge, while a mere starred rock turns out to be a 50-yard whaleback of sullen dry stone.*

*The GPS wasn't useful for navigating; there's no use knowing where you are if you don't know what's around you, but it was good to be able to record the locations of things they found.*[38]

They anchored each night around 10:00, and were underway again at 4:30 or 5:00 a.m., the captain or mate glued to the radar or depth sounder.[39] They followed the single track of soundings on the chart as closely as they could, but as Chase wrote,

*Every once in a while there would be a rude surprise as the fathometer shot up from 30 fathoms to ten, or once, five . . . [setting] a routine of running the engine at 1250 rpm when the depth was more than 20 fathoms; under 20, reduced to 1000 rpm; below 10, matched the depth in fathoms to the rpms (at 7 fathoms, ran the engine at 700 rpms.) Below five was idle, anything below four was stop or back full. The real problem is when you find it so shallow, you don't know which way to turn.*[40]

The *Bowdoin* continued on down the Labrador coast, to Nain. When the barometer again was dropping, Elliot wrote, "We have by this point become almost blasé about watching the changes in the weather and are simply responding to them. . . . The transitions are so abrupt and erratic that it is useless to do much else."[41]

Tom and Steve left the schooner at Nain, and six New England canoeists came aboard to describe their adventures. Through the Strait of Belle Isle, more gales arose. Finally, at Cape Breton, there was the first warm weather. Here, the *Bowdoin*'s World War II skipper joined the crew: Captain Stuart Hotchkiss, now age 78. People gathered around him at breakfast, lunch, and supper as he told of the differences on the *Bowdoin* between 1991 and how he remembered her in 1942.[42]

East of Halifax, Elliot wrote:

*The breeze has built to a near gale behind us and we are scream-ing along at 11 knots, as if the boat is ready to be home. . . . Carried the full mainsail well into the white knuckles zone, and finally replaced it with the trysail at 1900, still averaging 8 knots. Stu has been at the wheel most of the day, grinning like a fool. At 2130, Andy and I lean with tired elbows on a chart that, for the first time, contains home at the periphery. . . . On deck it has flattened out, the high moved in and the barograph steady. At sunset the sky was the color of pumpkin. Stu stood with a fishing rod, perhaps only slightly short of complete rapture. This man with five Navy commands has returned to delight us all.*[43]

The *Bowdoin*'s steadfast reliability, and the captain's thorough training of the crew, made the voyage less hazardous, although Elliot once described Andy, who "dives back into his bunk. He is a fixture there, writing letters . . . or reading an endless series of thick tomes about people who have gone to the Arctic and met with disaster."[44]

Likewise, MacMillan had also read about previous Arctic voyages on his off-duty time to educate himself about the region and its hazards and learn how difficulties had been resolved. Furthermore, it may have served as a conscious deterrent to relaxing the unremitting vigilance required to safely sail.[45]

*Bowdoin* Captain Andy Chase and his steward, Deborah Harrison, were temporarily disoriented as they docked in Bar Harbor, facing their reluctant entry back into the complex yet mundane civilized world. She wrote:

> *I see no joy in Andy's face at being back in 'civilization.' I thought I would be glad to be back. But there is no joy for him to see in my face, either. . . . I felt an overwhelming dread. What do we have in common with these people anymore? And then I felt we were losing something.*[46]

Elliot completed his journal at Mount Desert Island, writing:

> *There is a feeling of something finished, already drifting into the past. . . . To quantify our experience is impossible from such a short vantage, but the effort is made and the words are said. . . . Here's to the boat. Here's to eighty North. . . . The Dipper hangs in the sky, and a cold front whispers on the wind.*[47]

Although aboard the *Bowdoin* for sail training and numerous public relations tours, neither Chase nor Harrison has returned to the Arctic. But for the *Bowdoin's* first mate on both the 1990 and 1991 voyages, Elliot Rappaport, it is a different story.

First Mate Elliot Rappaport of Maine Maritime Academy accompanied Captain Andy Chase on the *Bowdoin* as she returned to the Arctic for the two voyages in 1990 and 1991, the first since Admiral MacMillan in 1954. He became her next skipper when she returned again three years later. He wrote,

*In 1994, it was decided to take the vessel to the Arctic again, using the experience gained in 1991 to expand the scope of the cruise track, going farther north, and spending more time on the Greenland coast. The educational plan was similar to that begun by MacMillan and continued on 1990 and 1991 cruises—students would acquire hands on experience as active watch members and receive supplemental information from a daily schedule of lectures and drills. Each trainee would also be required to design and complete an independent research project related to the cruise.*[48]

On July 2, Captain Rappaport commanded the *Bowdoin* as she left Castine, bound for Greenland and the Arctic. Ten trainees were along, only one of them from Maine Maritime Academy, and a 1991 crew member, the photographer Tom Stewart.[49] Elliot gave a review of the schooner's itinerary:

Bowdoin *lies dressed in flags and surrounded by an astonishing pile of stores and equipment, ready to return to the Arctic.* Bowdoin's *route would follow a track similar to those on many of her previous northern voyages: northeast from Maine to St. Johns, Newfoundland, and then 1,000 miles due north across the Labrador Sea to Nuuk, Latitude 64' 10", capitol and primary settlement of Greenland. The schooner would then continue northward as far as time and ice conditions allowed before transiting the Davis Strait and returning home via the Labrador coast.*[50]

On the 1994 voyage, the weather was mostly just cold and wet and dreary, Elliot reports. However, July 17 brought a day of Force 10 winds in the Labrador Sea. Elliot describes the event:

*At this latitude, in the summertime, the light clings to the night sky like a coat of bioluminescent moss, a cold blue glow thrown up into the firmament from somewhere below the horizon. The sea surface is black, and the omnipresent clouds of fog are cold as billows of vapor from a walk in freezer.*[51]

Later that night, he continues,

*At 0215, a watch officer, wearing enough outerwear for a walk in space, came below to tell me that the wind, steady from the southwest for the last 24 hours, had gone light, and started to veer. The barometer, at 29.35, had fallen from 30.00 over a similar interval. With a watch change upcoming, we shortened the sail to trysail, foresail, and staysail. By 0300, the wind had built to Force 6 from the north, and by 0430 to Force 8, at which point the fore was struck. The trysail, as if to protest, blew out its clew cringle and was taken down as well.*

*The 0700 watch change found us hove to on the starboard tack, with the staysail aback, and the engine slow ahead. This left the* Bowdoin *riding with the developing seas coming about two points forward of the beam, and the vessel making slight headway to the westward, a track we figured to be opposite that of the system. Conditions had built to a steady Force 8, with gusts to 10. Under an imperceptible brightening of the sky, the sea surface changed color from black to grey, riven into white streaks by the wind.*

*The air temperature dropped from 8.5 to around 4 Celsius, slightly colder than the seawater. In the near freezing rain, I stood on deck and wondered why anyone would build an Arctic schooner without a pilothouse.*

*In the middle of it all, half a dozen pilot whales leapt out horizontally from the face of a towering wave, as if to join us on the quarterdeck. The water looked the color of jade, and the animals close enough to touch as they went by.*[52]

Elliot further adds:

*Word of this particular blow reached Castine, and upon our return in September, somebody sent a card, congratulating us on a safe trip, and adding rather glibly, ". . . but what's 50 knots? We do it all the time!" In hindsight, I think that what separated the trip from much that I'd experienced elsewhere was the pervasive cold, an element that adds to the normal hazards of heavy weather the dangers of hypothermia, especially on a vessel with no shelter on deck. The challenges of sailing a traditional vessel offshore, handling sails, lines, and gear, of staying alert and watchful, of looking out for yourself and your watchmates, are all made far more difficult with the addition of constantly cold fingers, and heavy layers of clothing. The notion that crews routinely worked vessels like this one in all weathers and seasons becomes all the more impressive.*[53]

Afterward, as Sid Clemens, a blue water sailor and 1994 *Bowdoin* trainee affirmed, "Even in a full gale, when you couldn't open your eyes on deck, she rode beautifully. She's perfect for what she's doing."[54]

The 1991 voyage had taken the schooner 150 miles north of the Arctic Circle. Elliot met his goal of extending the *Bowdoin*'s range by 85 miles to 71 degrees 25 minutes North at the Umanak Fjord. On July 21 in Davis Strait, Elliot wrote:

*We have so much more than MacMillan had—electronics, Mustang suits, GPS. The exotic wireless that once filled a cabin is now a commonplace retail item the size of a shoebox. But we keep the cold and damp, the dreary half-nights of these latitudes, the hours of staring myopically into gray mist. And we keep a feeling that was surely there before—that slight sense of foreboding, of sailing north into a barren world through a tiny window of summer.*

*It is a land of anachronisms. The Inuit population lived an itinerant existence based around hunting and fishing. Today, the place is in the middle of an identity crisis that is the result of trying to convert an Arctic colony into a modern Scandinavian welfare state, trying to move the world's hardiest and most enduring outdoor culture into apartment buildings. The outboard has replaced the kayak, and modern factory trawlers are attacking the fish stocks. Dogsleds sit in driveways next to modern four-wheel-drive vehicles. What remain are the Greenlandic language and the dietary culture of a population that still extracts much of its food from the environment. Those too busy to hunt their own seals and puffins can find them at the grocery store, next to melons imported from Israel.*

*In the town of Sisimiut, a local trawler captain took me into his modern Danish home, where, hanging above the stainless steel and leather couch, was a sealskin kayak his father had paddled nearly every day of his life.*[55]

Sailing in Davis Strait on July 27, Rappaport describes the ice surrounding the *Bowdoin*:

*The ice marches by in a monolithic parade of shapes—immense haystacks, meringues, sugar cubes, crystalline elephants, wrought with veins of re-frozen water. It is an almost implausible shade of blue. This afternoon, a berg that we'd just passed split into with a huge crack, and and dropped a garage sized piece of itself into the sea. In the still water, the splash produced a perfect curling wave of green. It looked like a surfing poster.*

*The bulk of icebergs in the North Atlantic are formed by the glaciers of West Greenland, with a handful near the 70th parallel accounting for most of the production. Some move a hundred feet per day and fill the fjords that lead up to them with a continuous stream of ice, sometimes so tightly jammed as to be unnavigable. Icebergs are current driven and ride the West Greenland and Labrador currents in a counterclockwise circumnavigation of the Labrador Sea before finally expiring near the Grand Banks, a process that takes one to three years.*

*Sea ice, or pack ice, covers Arctic waters in varying concentrations, generally reaching its peak in early spring. . . . The west coast of Greenland is passable by July, as are the coasts of Labrador and southern Baffin Island. Conditions vary year to year, and plans must be often be adjusted accordingly.*[56]

*In the low light of morning and evening, ice takes on the colors of apricot, and of rose quartz. The blues deepen and seem to irridesce. In photographs the colors are often so vivid that people assume they're enhanced, but the opposite is true: it is a rare image that can reproduce their intensity.*[57]

On August 1, near Karrats Fjord, West Greenland, Elliot describes the fjord in which the *Bowdoin* is sailing. He writes:

Bowdoin *seems to have wandered into a lake. Mile high peaks plunge down around us into a pool of still water, ringed by the tongues of hanging glaciers. . . . Several miles beyond, the passage*

*joins Kangerdlugsuaq Fjord. . . . The scale is so vast that the*
*features appear in full detail miles ahead, and the vista seems to*
*hang in freeze-frame for an hour, until suddenly we are there.*

*There is no sunset tonight, and the light grows longer and*
*longer. It is midnight. To our right, the Karrats Fjord comes into*
*view, a solid pile of bergs the size of soccer stadiums, lit the color*
*of peach. The breeze has dropped imperceptibly, and now there is*
*barely a ripple.*[58]

Elliot finishes his view of a magnificent vista of two fjords
merging together:

*It is odd how, in some instants, there is the feeling of arriving at*
*a place that was there waiting for you all along. I cannot imag-*
*ine that this place has ever looked much different. We tie up to*
*an iceberg. Shut down. Drink a toast of apple juice. A crew goes*
*ashore to build a cairn. It is a moment when people try to talk*
*and then go silent that seems to demand testimony and silence*
*simultaneously.*[59]

Two days later, in Illusisat, Greenland, Elliot records:

*The crew of the shrimper Assimiut gave us so much of their catch*
*that I fear for our stability, and then welcome us into their fo'c'sle*
*for a visit. They are on a 24-hour turnaround between six-day*
*trips, and sleep for them seems pointless.*

*The best charts of Greenland are Danish, beautiful things*
*printed on heavy stock in several colors. The information on them*
*is good, but they are cheated by the scale of the place they must*
*describe. The west coast, 1500 miles as the auk flies, is covered by*

*a mere two dozen charts. There are no buoys, few aids to navigation. Away from the approaches to primary harbors, inshore soundings break down into sparse chains of single numbers, or areas simply left blank.*

*Labrador is worse. Few people have had cause to travel here in the last fifty years, and the Northern charts . . . devoid of color, with few soundings and a scattering of information that is all bad news.*[60]

Elliot, however, sees the practical advantage of such a lack of indicators:

*Trainees benefited from situations that required them to take nothing for granted, and to employ all available information in navigating. Careful use of soundings and visual observations were required to verify (or add to) information all ready on the charts. The fathometer ran all summer, ticking like a metronome. It consumed reams of paper.*[61]

On August 13, at the Okak Islands, Labrador, his narrative is finally reminiscent of home:

*We raised the Labrador coast yesterday afternoon, black saw-toothed mountains on the edge of an afternoon sky that was suddenly sunlit and warm. The light came down from above, not sideways, threw shadows and gave out a whiff of forgotten summer. . . . Bowdoin ghosts through a landscape that is emptier than a school in summertime. . . . The trip down Labrador was a slow return to earth, interspersed with reminders of how far away home remained. . . . We saw trees today. . . . It got dark at night.*[62]

The schooner was at Nain, Labrador, on August 17.

*Labrador's northernmost surviving settlement is the archetype of the Canadian Arctic town. The way home on August 19 winds through the labyrinth of islands south of Nain in a series of endless turnings. Green and black hills rise like mountains breaking water. Only occasionally, when a reach opens to the eastwards and lets in the cold breath of the sea, does it seem possible that this place is connected to those we have been.*[63]

Nearing Penobscot Bay, Elliot reviews the assigned educational activities for the voyage:

*The Labrador coast reaches its southern extremity at Red Bay, and by August 30, we were roaring across the Lakes of Cape Breton, before a stiff, dry westerly. Students presented their projects and struggled to hold notes. Efforts from 1994 include studies of ocean currents, shipboard psychology, Inuit spiritual culture, and a project designed to study the viability of homeopathic medical treatment for the offshore sailor.*[64]

With the schooner in home port on September 3 in Castine, he finalizes the *Bowdoin's* 21st Arctic voyage:

*After pushing through headwinds for the final 48 hours, end of the cruise ceremonies were conducted on the fly, as the summer abandoned two months before resumed unaltered. In Penobscot Bay, the small, spruce covered islands looked almost lush.*

*There is a sense after a voyage that somehow things will change after returning, as if to mirror the miles traveled. Often as not, what is found instead is the closing of a circle, a sense of having completed a loop that takes you back almost to where you began. It is from here, that the challenge of assimilating life into experience begins. In Castine, there are the same loved ones, the same dockside watchers, and Labrador retrievers. The lines that came aboard two months ago are thrown back onto the float and land with a bass thump.*

*4,500 miles, 64 days, and 320 watch changes. 1,536 boat checks, 35 pounds of lentils. Behind us, the eastern headland of Castine Harbor blocks our last view to the open sea.*

In the 1994 voyage, the highlight of the voyage for many, including Elliot, was Farthest North: Umanak Fjord, at 71 degrees 25 minutes. Elliot says this region, with its many glaciers is the most spectacular place he's ever been. The drama of the scenery jumps by another exponent from Disko Bay. The *Bowdoin* was 85 miles north of her extreme of Chase's 1991 trip, fulfilling Elliot's dream of expanding his range with the schooner.

Looking back at the docked schooner riding quietly on the harbor waters, one imagines she is only stationary until tomorrow morning, when a crew boards her and begins another passage. Writing afterward, Elliot declared, "There's a difference between a schooner that goes to the Arctic, and one that has been to the Arctic."

Captain Rappaport later joined the Sea Education Association in 2001 at Woods Hole, Massachusetts, and finally returned to the academy in the fall of 2019. Now a professor, his courses include Seamanship, Marine Communications, and Small Craft Construction.

Everyone who knows the *Bowdoin* understands that the Northern expeditions are an essential function of the schooner.

Nevertheless, over fourteen years would pass before the schooner set sail for the Arctic again.

She finally returned in 2008, when Captain Richard (Rick) Miller in the *Bowdoin* crossed the Arctic Circle for the fourth time since MacMillan in 1954. He commanded the schooner on her most recent return to the Arctic, after serving as chief mate with his predecessor, Captain John Worth.

Leaving Castine on May 29, 2008, with sixteen academy students, their first port was St. Johns, Newfoundland, and then they revisited Chase and Rappaport's ports of call. They reached Farthest North, 66 degrees 31 minutes, at Illusiat, Greenland. Told that the port was iced in, but seeing a vessel come out, Captain Miller entered, but was unable to leave, as the wind had come out of the west, closing the harbor entrance with ice.

The master of a Danish cruise ship entered the harbor, and while talking with Rick, mentioned that he had sailed aboard the *Danmark*. Rick gave him a tour of the *Bowdoin*, and admitted he was unsure how he would leave. The captain told Miller to follow him out the next day, claiming, "Stay on our stern; we'll get you out." After 4 miles in his path, Captain Miller was able to turn north, and sail to Disko Island. He returned to Castine on August 8.

His assessment of the *Bowdoin* was that she is an "amazing vessel." Formerly an instructor with Outward Bound, Rick is now a professor in the academy's Transportation Department, instructing Celestial Navigation and Marine Weather Routing. He is comfortable in a variety of ship handling positions. In the summer, he instructs college courses aboard the Woods Hole Sea Education Association brigantine S/V *Robert E. Seamans*.

# 9

# Making Headway

*The* Bowdoin *is worth our investment. She continues to work hard in support of the training mission of the school and serves as an ambassador for Maine Maritime Academy wherever she sails. Most importantly,* Bowdoin *offers an experience rich in maritime tradition and teamwork for our sail training students.*
—CAPTAIN ERIC JERGENSEN, 2014

BEGINNING IN 1989, MAINE MARITIME ACADEMY INITIATED A new curriculum for sail training, leading to a two- or four-year degree, the sole sailing degree program at the maritime academies in the United States. When purchased, the *Bowdoin* was intended to develop the program, as well as serve as a sailing ambassador, among other educational activities. Realizing that the

*use of traditional sailing vessels in education has its roots in the days of working sail, and endures at many international maritime academies, where a cruise on a sail training vessel is required for graduation. Trainees aboard such vessels profit from an exposure to the marine environment unbuffered by the amenities in modern ships. Watches are kept on an open deck, and careful teamwork is necessary in order to handle sail. Long passages require careful study of wind and weather patterns, and the working of the vessel imparts a sense of shared responsibility—a feeling often obscured on larger craft.*[1]

The Nautical Science department at the academy emphasizes the schooner's use. After the return voyages to the Arctic in 1990 and crossing the Arctic Circle in 1991, 1994, and 2008, where "the challenge of operating a traditionally rigged vessel in Arctic waters, combined with the historical connections between *Bowdoin* and the north, proved to be a superb foundation for a sail training program."[2]

The program was further expanded:

*In the seasons of 1992 and 1993, the educational focus was brought closer to home. Shorter programs in seamanship and ocean studies were developed, along with a series of three-day trips for students and teachers from Maine's secondary schools. In the fall,* Bowdoin *continued to serve the mainstream academy curricula, providing daily and weekend cruises for trainees in nautical science, ocean studies and small vessel operations.*[3]

In 2009, Eric Jergensen (MMA '12), while attending the academy in the Sail Training Program, sailed as crew aboard the *Bowdoin*, filling positions from deckhand to sailing master. He holds a license for Auxiliary Sailing Vessels for All Oceans, and is a U.S. Sailing Certified Coastal Passage Instructor and an Instructor Trainer for Basic Keelboat and Cruising Instructors.

In the spring of 2014, while sailing *Bowdoin* on a public relations tour to Portland, Maine, and Provincetown, Massachusetts, Captain Jergensen discovered a potential compromise in the mainmast during a routine rigging check. He suspended sailing and contacted the academy. It happened on the first day of the week, and by midweek, a shipwright was aboard the schooner to conduct an in-depth inspection of the mast. Due to the inspection results, Jergensen decided not to continue sailing until repairs were made.[4]

He apologized to the Portland and Provincetown connections and promised to return soon. Jergensen and his crew assisted in the construction of the new mast, built by Andros Kypragoras Shipbuilding, Inc. It was completed in 45 days. On August 15, the newly constructed laminated mast, inspected and approved by the USCG, was installed. Eric praised everyone involved: "You made this happen. Thanks for your hard work and long hours. This mast is better than the last! To all who care about *Bowdoin,* and her important mission at Maine Maritime Academy, thank you for your support."[5]

This was the *Bowdoin's* fifth mast, replacing the mast made and donated by the Weyerhauser Company in 1976, which had been installed after Jim Sharp's mast broke off at the crosstrees and was hastily rebuilt using a large pipe at Billings Diesel in Stonington.

Captain Jergensen was able to keep his training cruise as scheduled that weekend, carrying eleven rising seniors to Nova Scotia and back. The *Bowdoin's* itinerary was:

August 11–22: Cruise to Nova Scotia, with visits to Halifax, Lunenburg, and Shelburne.

August 22–29: Return to Castine.[6]

It has been found that on cloudy days, in stormy weather, or with the loss of power or satellite coverage electronic communication is adversely affected. The old ways of dead reckoning (DR), sextant use, and knowledge of manual skills becomes mandatory. The U.S. Coast Guard's Standards of Training, Certification and Watchkeeping (STCW) are requisite, and the Transportation faculty at the Academy remain adamant proponents.

Jergensen is now a professor at the academy in the Transportation Department. In the fall of 2020, he taught Natural Navigation, a course presenting the historic view of the traditional method of navigation before the advent of accurate charts, the development of the sextant, and inventions of the modern LORAN and GPS. When both of the *Bowdoin*'s compasses failed after an electrical storm on her second voyage in 1923–1924, MacMillan relied on this method, advocating as essential.

Jergensen's 2020 spring semester courses include Seamanship, Celestial Navigation, and the Electronic Navigation Lab. Eric is also the founder of the Maine Ocean School, a secondary level charter school in its second year in Searsport. The school offers marine-oriented courses in the required academic basics, preparing students for admission to a college degree program in various maritime fields of study.

The Sailing Program at the academy is the only degree program in the United States. The four-year program fulfills the requirements for the bachelor of science degree in Vessel Operations and Technology (VOT) leading to a 500-ton or 1600-ton (depending on the seatime accrued by the candidate) mate's USCG license. The associate degree in Small Vessel Operations (SVO) leads to a 200-ton USCG license as a mate on an auxiliary sail vessel. The *Bowdoin*, the first vessel to be certified under the United States Sail Training Act in 1986, is the flagship of the academy's sail training program.[7]

It is fitting that the first graduate of the VOT program in 2012, with USCG certification for the 1600-ton mate's license, is Captain Will McLean, now the schooner's master.[8] While at Maine Maritime, he served as a mate and bosun for Captain John Worth, graduating from Maine Maritime Academy as a USCG-licensed mate on all levels.

Captain McLean continued accumulating further experience on the tall ship *Pride of Baltimore II* and as senior chief mate/relief captain for three years on the SSV *Robert E. Seamans* for the Sea Education Association in Woods Hole.[9] He completed a winter sail in the Sea of Cortez as captain of the classic 82-foot staysail schooner *Seaward* with the Call of the Sea, an educational non-profit dedicated to environmental education through sailing. Will took command of the *Bowdoin* on May 8, 2017.[10]

Captain Dana Willis, the academy's Waterfront Operations Manager emphasized the *Bowdoin's* importance at the academy: "As the flagship of our sail training program, *Bowdoin* is an extremely important vessel in our fleet."[11]

Praising Will, he said, "I am extremely pleased to welcome Will to the helm, because he epitomizes the dedication of our faculty and alumni; he is passionate about sail training and also has a great interest in mentoring and educating students."[12]

Captain McLean responded:

*I am excited to return to Maine Maritime as a Captain, and to have the opportunity to work with students learning and sailing on the* Bowdoin. *We get started on our first training voyage in a few weeks and before we head offshore we'll be training the new crew on the traditional skills of handling sail, reefing, and steering the ship through the beautiful passages found along Penobscot Bay.*[13]

Sara Martin was selected by McLean as the *Bowdoin's* chief mate in 2020.

Summer sail training cruises—the CR 214 Auxiliary Sail Training Cruise, taught in part on the *Bowdoin* by Captain McLean, and CR 313 Small Vessel Operations Sail Training Cruise, taught exclusively on the *Bowdoin* by Captain Andy Chase—incorporate all the traditional and modern aspects of seamanship. Senior students effectively finish their studies aboard the *Bowdoin*. Captain McLean wrote in a 2019 issue of *The Mariner*:

> *After 31 years of service as MMA's sail training vessel, schooner* Bowdoin *was back in blue water this summer for her 98th year of sailing. . . .* Bowdoin *recently completed her annual training cruises to the Canadian Maritimes. . . . The recent restoration could not have been done without . . . the amazing outpouring of support from previous* Bowdoin *captains, crew, friends and MMA alumni.*[14]

It is well known that sailing is a fundamental skill and vital for safety for any seaman. Almost everyone has experienced sailing in small boats on lakes or bays in their early years.

According to Jack Frazier (MMA '21), a sail training student from Washington State, the Puget Sound Pilot Association recommends sail training not only for traditional sailors and tall-ship personnel but for captains and pilots of propulsion-driven vessels as well.[15]

Furthermore, the managements of modern ports have acknowledged the necessity of promoting the importance of sail training as an asset to the education of a pilot, captain, and all crew members, due to the thorough understanding of the wind's effects and influence on vessel control a sailor routinely gains. The hull of an enormous tanker presents a surface nearly as impacted by the wind as a full sail.

Importantly, former sail training student Eric Romelczyk (MMA '08) reflects:

*Standing watch in the wheelhouse of a modern commercial vessel may not seem to have much to do with the quarterdeck of a historic sailing vessel, but the environment we all operate in offers the same challenges. There is no better place to develop the intuitive "feel" for managing the interaction of wind, water on your hull than on the open deck of a vessel powered by the wind.*[16]

When he assumed command of the *Bowdoin* in May, Captain McLean's teaching duties began immediately. Students in the sail training program begin Basic Sailing instruction and Seamanship on one design sailboats such as the two-man Mercury16. Also, they experience day sails on the *Bowdoin* and may join the sailing team, learning sail handling for competition. In 2021, the academy's varsity sailing team travels to California to participate in an International Sailing Competition.

Following mastery of the 16s, students graduate to the larger Colgate 26s. In Intermediate Sailing, they practice more complex maneuvers, including heaving to and man-overboard drills.

In Advanced Sailing, students gain more experience in an assortment of keel boats and larger sailboats. They progress to the academy's Sidney 38' and the 42' wooden schooner, the *Puritan*. They learn the skills to repair and maintain the vessel, including traditional rigging, leatherwork, caulking, and sail making and repair. They practice more challenging activities, from navigation and standing watch to the vessel operations of tacking and jibing.[17]

All students eventually prepare, train, and sail on the 88'*Bowdoin*. In addition to being the ultimate sail training vessel, the schooner *Bowdoin* is a Tall Ship, Class B. Captain Andy Chase explains that tall ships are *complex, and every task on board is critical. Mistakes can be dangerous, with a potential for serious damage if not handled properly. The training offered through the* Bowdoin's *Leadership Lab produces mariners who can accomplish tasks smoothly, swiftly, safely, and as part of a team. The basic fundamental seamanship skills along with the historical context provided to the students in a necessarily collaborative setting makes a tall ship, like the* Bowdoin, *ideal for such training.*[18]

*Every evolution on a sailing vessel requires a team working together at the direction of a trained leader. To raise a sail, to tack, to jibe, or to strike sail, to reef, or to shake out a reef, requires a group of people to be led in a coordinated effort with great care for safety. The* Bowdoin's *size means that nearly everyone on board is either involved in the process, or within sight of it, observing and learning. Experienced crew are there to demonstrate and model the process, and after a time, the trainees can step in and lead the evolution themselves.*[19]

*A mariner's business is seamanship. And there may be no better place to learn than the* Bowdoin.[20]

The *Bowdoin*'s summer training cruises are invaluable, and available to trainees in all levels of the program. While the Sail Training Program is constantly developing, since every student needs a challenge, and the *Bowdoin* challenges each student differently. The captain is there to ensure that nothing goes wrong and to

- give feedback
- emphasize critical thinking
- participate in useful conversation
- help students learn about mariners' mistakes [21]

As an alumni of Captain McLean's CR-214 course, one student noted: "CR-214 gave me practical skills that set me up for success in my navigation classes on campus."[22]

Every cruise aboard the *Bowdoin* is a singular experience. Students are under the guidance of one of the academy's captains; and while each captain has specific expertise, all the seamanship elements are emphasized. Along with the training cruises and daily sailing, the schooner is an essential part of any related event.

For example, *Bowdoin* participated in the July 2014 gathering of sailing vessels designed by William H. and R. O. Davis. On display were the *Bowdoin, Burma, Guildive,* and *Tracker,* which were constructed between 1921 and 1950. They met at Portland, and all vessels were open for daylong inspection to the public, educating those interested in the designers' work, especially in the world-famous schooner *Bowdoin.*

In 2015, *Bowdoin* led the Parade of Tall Ships at Portland, Maine, and attended the Tall Ships Rendevous in Quebec City in 2017. Captain McLean and his crew won the Best Crew Award for the *Bowdoin*'s excellent condition.

Additionally, the schooner's Arctic activities are ongoing in associated events and developments. Tours of the schooner were available on July 10, 2015, as the Fulbright Scholars Program presented seminars on the Arctic and climate change in the morning. Captain Rick Miller spoke on "Arctic Sailing on the *Bowdoin*: Memoirs of a Captain" after dinner. The Maine chapter of the Fulbright Association hosted the presentation at the college.

The next year, the *Bowdoin* carried participants in the Arctic Command on October 4, 2016, from Castine and was docked at the USCG mooring on Wright's Wharf in Portland for tours. The schooner was met by members of the Arctic Council, representing countries from across the globe. Admiral Robert J. Papp and Dr.

William Brennan, the college's president, were joined by two Arctic Youth Ambassadors from Alaska, and fourteen Maine students from Baxter Academy for Technology and Science in Portland

Admiral Papp (USCG Ret.), the U.S. Special Representative for the Arctic, is leading the effort to advance U.S. interests in the Arctic. His focus is on the Arctic Ocean stewardship, climate change, and the economic, environmental, and security issues in the Arctic region. He and President Brennan spoke at the meeting.

The United States held the Chairmanship of the Arctic Council from 2015 to 2017. In 2016 the Ice Training requirements of the International Marine Organization (IMO) Polar Code were established. The academy will be assisted with environmental oversight by the North American Marine Environmental Protection Association.

Admiral MacMillan commissioned and explored the Arctic with his schooner. He presented the *Bowdoin* in his educational and scientific studies and lectures after her Arctic voyages. As a result, the schooner's consequence is noteworthy and an invaluable link to the past and future history of the Arctic.

As one of the eight Arctic nations, the United States, along with Canada, Russia, Norway, Sweden, Finland, Iceland, and Denmark, is a permanent member of the Arctic Council, since it owns territory north of the Arctic Circle. The nations represent competitive interests in the Arctic's natural resources. The environment there is challenging—physically, economically, and politically. According to the Coast Guard, the long-term goal is a safe, secure Arctic that is in political, economic, and environmental balance.

Toward this end, a $250,000 grant from the Department of Homeland Security was awarded, with $187,000 for education. In preparation for warmer temperatures opening the Arctic to transportation, Polar Exploration electives, the only such courses available on the college level, are taught at the academy by Transportation Professor Captain Ralph Pundt. His prior shipping experience included delivering oil and supplies to MacMurdo Station in Antarctica, Terra Nova in Newfoundland, and Toulee, Greenland.

Courses on the basic and advanced levels are offered every other year to academy students. At the college's Continuing Education Center in Bucksport, Polar Exploration courses are held regularly for recertification.

Learners in Basic Polar Exploration have 40 hours of lecture, must meet the STCW requirements, and must pass a final exam. The Advanced Polar Exploration course also meets the STCW requirements, includes simulator training with ice driving instruction, and ends in certification through the USCG Exam. Captain McLean and the chief mate will be certified at the advanced level before they return to the Arctic on the centennial voyage.

Approximately 95 percent of the world's goods travel by water. Although the United States is now 28th in standing in the world fleet, twenty U.S.-flagged vessels still transport a variety of materials, including foreign aid across the globe, with commerce remaining of major consequence. Additionally, sail and passenger trade has increased, as well as research and exploration.

The *Bowdoin* represents this last area, and has participated for a century in all aspects, extraordinary for an active wooden vessel. Each decade has shown her adaptation to modern requirements, inventions, and improvements. Her accomplishments befit an historic past and are significant for the future. The skills and care of her captains show the abilities of the vessel, and her potential reiterates more possible prospects, only limited by the events in which she will be the focus.

In education, Captain John Murray (MMA '79) sees that "success in today's industry isn't limited to shipboard skills. There are great opportunities ashore for those willing to work hard and apply their classroom learning and experiences to building great maritime careers."

He is a 40-year maritime industry veteran who oversees the port of Cape Canaveral in Florida. Concerned about all aspects of merchant shipping, Murray addressed Congress in 2016 to provide details on the challenges of sustaining the fleet due to reduced food aid cargoes, earmarked for U.S. flag transport:

*We're down to about eighty American flagged deep-sea cargo vessels; sixty of them are in the Maritime Security Program with the balance in the Jones Act domestic trades. In times of national emergency, trained and experienced U. S. mariners are needed, but the size of the American fleet and employment opportunities are not adequate, and the economics of maintaining these ships and a pool of skilled mariners has become more difficult. Year after year, I have seen support chipping away.*

Globally, the period from 2020 to 2030 has been designated by the United Nations as the Decade of Ocean Literacy, as we seek to further understand, protect, and utilize the seas. Advances in this decade will be of interest to more than just the Arctic states and will affect the world.

IV

# On a Reach

Fair Winds and Following Seas

# The Centennial

Bowdoin *is a very special ship. . . . Being able to keep her story alive is something I will never forget. It is so important that Maine Maritime Academy is successful with campaigns such as this to preserve our country's rich maritime history for generations to come.*

—*BOWDOIN* CENTENNIAL CAMPAIGN
CO-CHAIRMAN ALEX WATSON, 2015

KEN CURTIS, MAINE MARITIME ACADEMY PRESIDENT FROM 1985 to 1994, wrote, "We are a small college with the largest campus in the world –the Atlantic Ocean."[1] In 1988, President Curtis became responsible for bringing the *Bowdoin* and her assets to the college through the petition of a student, Chris Kluck.

The United States is a maritime nation—historically, culturally, and economically. Our inimitable maritime background is the foundation, requisite for those in the sea services, including the merchant marine.

Therefore, it seems inconsistent that the academy is the only one of the six public maritime academies that does not offer Maritime Literature and Maritime History as required liberal arts courses in the curriculum, along with the current variety of electives. These subjects are the indispensable background in support of the maritime STEM subjects taught at the academy and provide important content and references. Academy graduates should have the knowledge and awareness of most mariners in this regard.

Maritime Literature, in all its many expressions, is the epitome of critical thinking. Problem solving, decision making, creativity, evaluation, and metacognitive examination are the distinguishing attributes of the successful captain, first mate, officers, and the crew members down to the steward, in both nonfiction and fiction. Maritime History describes the major events in the development of America, the result of our maritime influence, and the ensuing accomplishments that form the base of our country's history.

Moreover, docked at the academy's waterfront is an authentic example: the *Bowdoin*—her creation, voyages of exploration and discovery, as well as longevity—with public awareness and support as confirmation. Established as the first USCG Certified Sail Training Vessel in 1986, the Maine Official State Vessel in 1988, and as a United States Historical Landmark in 1989, her qualifications present unmistakable verification.

Moreover, the course catalog of the academy describes the college's mission as the instruction of courses "primarily focused on marine related programs."[2] Regardless of trends, and with certification enforced by the United States Coast Guard, every maritime academy endeavors to produce some of the most skillful mariners in the world. Central to the academy's sail training program leading to a professional mariner's license are the college's sailing vessels, led by the *Bowdoin*.

As the highlight of the Arctic schooner's centennial festivities in 2021, a commemorative Arctic voyage was planned, the *Bowdoin*'s fifth from Maine Maritime Academy.[3] In light of her ongoing contributions, the schooner *Bowdoin*—an ideal example for instructing sailing, seamanship, and navigation—is an important factor in promoting the Arctic.[4]

Among many other interesting centennial activities, a panel of *Bowdoin*'s past and present captains met to reminisce about the schooner and the voyages they commanded.

## The *Bowdoin*'s Captains at Maine Maritime Academy: 1988–Present

1988–1991: Captain Andy Chase
   Two voyages:
   1990 to Nain, Labrador
   1991: 150 miles above the Arctic Circle

1992–2001: Captain Elliot Rappaport
   Longest serving captain of the *Bowdoin* except MacMillan
   Rebuilt the *Bowdoin*'s galley and interior
   1994: Sailed 85 miles further than Chase above the Arctic Circle

2002–2003: Captain Heather Stone

2004–2009: Captain John Worth

2007–2009: Captain Richard Miller
   2008: Most recent voyage to the Arctic Circle

2009–2016: Captain Eric Jergensen
   Replaced *Bowdoin*'s mainmast, her fifth, in 2016

2015–2016: Captain Alec Schoettle

2016–2017: Captain Emma Hathaway

2017–Present: Captain Will McLean, Arctic Commemorative Voyage from 2021–202?
    2017: Oversaw deck rebuild at Wayfarer Marine in Camden
    2019: Oversaw hull rebuild at Bristol Boatyard in Boothbay Harbor
    2021–2022: Arctic Centennial Voyage

Other parts of the centennial events included ongoing showings of movies and an exhibit of photographs, including some of Mac-Millan's, as well as tours of the ship. (Appropriately, a portion of the sales of this volume will be donated to the vessel's Centennial Fund.)

While one may contend the theory that a ship is a living being, the schedule of events is confirmation. Many activities fill her hours to continue the justification for her presence at the academy. The sail training program alone is sufficient, as is the need for a good-will ambassador. In short, the schooner is both remarkable in her seaworthiness and longevity, from which all students can benefit.

# Wing and Wing

*She's exceptionally maneuverable, due to her perfect size.*
—Captain Will McLean

It is apparent in which direction the future of the *Bowdoin* lies. MacMillan asserted that "from the beginning, the *Bowdoin* was an exploratory vessel, sort of a floating science laboratory. Now it became a classroom as well."[1]

Her stability and flexibility provide a reliable medium, even in inclement weather and difficult circumstances, for instructing seamanship, developing students' experience, and accumulating sea time. Former summer student aboard the *Bowdoin* Aaron Grainnik stated:

> *My first real watch leadership was on* Bowdoin. *I loved the challenge of unplugging from all the screens, and just relying on the feel of the vessel and the environment around me.* Bowdoin's *focus on the cores of seamanship are still vital and prevalent in today's modern fleet.*[2]

Large enough to be seaworthy yet small enough to be easily handled, the schooner offers the opportunity for swift familiarity with the skills and practice of seamanship, as well as comparative ease in guiding her through every nautical event she encounters.

Through the years, her skippers have attested to the *Bowdoin*'s consistency; and an ever-increasing number of supporters who have seen and experienced her have become advocates, promoting her attributes and sponsoring her preservation.

In the fall of 2019, Maine Maritime Academy President William Brennan requested that a committee be formed to create a plan for the *Bowdoin*'s "ongoing maintenance and future restoration needs."[3] The committee members included current *Bowdoin* Captain Will McLean, Captain Eric Jergensen, Captain Rick Miller, Captain Zander Parker, Professor Kirk Langford, Professor Mark Shaughnessy, Captain Andy Chase, Captain Dana Willis, Yacht Donation Program Manager Joe Lobley, and Vice President for Advancement Chris Haley.[4]

By 2019 at Maine Maritime Academy, nearly $1.6 million in gifts, gifts in kind, and pledges had been donated over the past three years to fund the renovation and provide an endowment for maintenance of the schooner.[5] Supplemented with an additional $2 million over two years from the general funds allocated to the academy by the Maine State Legislature, the full renovation of her decks in 2017 at Wayfarer Marine (now Lyman Morse) in Camden and her hull replacement at Bristol Marine in Boothbay Harbor completed her restoration in the summer of 2019.

In the 2020 Issue 1 of the college journal *The Mariner*, Captain Chase stated that adequate funds, estimated at approximately $50,000 yearly, to keep the schooner ship shape are now available from the $1 million endowment raised.[6] The *Bowdoin* Centennial Campaign fund-raising was successful and the endowment goal was reached—in part through the unprecedented assistance of former student Jeffrey Pollock (MMA '15), who graduated from the academy with a master's degree in Global Logistics and Maritime Management.

He learned about the schooner's importance when he enrolled in the Applied Research for Business Consulting course, and selected the *Bowdoin* and the *Pentagoet* to study their impact on waterfront classes. Afterward, he chose, through funding from his uncle's bequest, to give $500,000 to the Centennial Campaign.[7]

Pollock remarked, "I love sailing, and just knowing a little bit about the history of the *Bowdoin* I thought we could keep this classic wooden boat sailing." This gift is the largest single contribution to Maine Maritime Academy by a student.[8] Such is the schooner's ability to inspire.

The able and historical *Bowdoin*'s contributions are described in the second 2015 issue of *The Mariner*, as the Centennial Campaign was launched. Centennial Campaign cochairman Captain Andy Chase said:

> *When you are immersed in, and at the mercy of the forces of nature, you must learn to observe them and predict them. You can't afford not to pay attention. The* Bowdoin *teaches these basics and teaches a rich lesson in maritime history and Arctic exploration. Our Centennial Campaign will ensure that she continues to be available for generations to come.*[9]

Captain Chase anticipates that the *Bowdoin* will continue to sail in her various capacities. He further outlined the funds available for her upkeep, including income from her $1 million endowment and the labor of her crew and academy students and faculty; as well as additional income from the charter of a mega-yacht recently given to the college.[10] Notably, the gift of another large yacht to the academy in 1988—which was sold—allowed the college to purchase the *Bowdoin*.

Captain Chase contends:

*With the rebuild, the* Bowdoin *is stronger than ever. We plan to take her back to the Arctic in 2021. She'll be closing the loop and continuing a 100-year record of environmental and cultural changes in the Arctic begun by MacMillan.*[11] . . . *We can sleep soundly knowing not only that we restored the* Bowdoin *once but will be able to do so again when needed, ensuring her longevity well past our lifetime.*

The *Bowdoin* will continue to sail as a training ship, the integral and definitive part of the college sailing program; a state and national ambassador; as well as an active historical artifact. She will be viewed as a noteworthy asset and a privilege to own, sail, and participate in the exclusive education for future generations of academy students.

Fortunately, the minutes of the last meeting in February 2020, of the Maine Maritime Academy Board of Trustees contain the funding report by Captain Chase with the request that the board accept the endowment for her care, specifically written so that the funds accompany the *Bowdoin* and remain dedicated exclusively to her.[13] The trustees accepted.

The *Bowdoin* is worthy of both dedication and attention, as successfully proven throughout her first century. Due to unprecedented circumstances in 2020, she was unable to complete her usual full summer of required cruises to provide the necessary instruction and sea time for sailors in training. To remedy this, additional cruises were scheduled at the completion of the 2021 spring semester, consisting of four training voyages in the Canadian Maritimes, currently under way.

Now, she revels in the student training voyages, punctuated by the occasional, too brief, afternoon sailing cruises commanded by the academy captains outside Castine Harbor, filled with faculty, guests, friends, and local admirers.

On the afternoon of September 17, 2020, she embarked from her berth at the academy's waterfront and the schooner quietly motored into Castine Harbor. First, she manuevered 360 degrees, then, raising full sail, glided past the 500-foot T/S *State of Maine* through a lightly rippling sea to the mouth of the Penobscot, stirring the bystanders' affection. She is not only a solidly impressive vessel, but a lovely sight with gleaming white sides, and tall dark masts adorned with five flags.

By late November, the *Bowdoin* will be prepared and covered, where she would rest at the academy dock with a weather eye open for the coming winter. In April, she will be uncovered in the northern sunlight, to welcome the arrival of spring, the beginning of a new season, and on April 9, 2021, the commencement of her second century.

# EPILOGUE

*Though much is taken, much abides and though*
*We are not now that strength which in old days*
*Moved heaven and earth, that which we, we are;*
*One equal temper of heroic hearts*
*Made weak by time and fate, but strong in will*
*To strive, to seek, to find, and not to yield.*
　　　　　—From "Ulysses" by Alfred, Lord Tennyson

After the 2019 rebuild, the *Bowdoin*'s strength returned to that of "old days," and she remains "strong in will." The *Bowdoin*, with care, will endure another 100 years with the temper and leadership of "heroic hearts," and her ability "to strive, to seek, to find, and not to yield."[1]

It has been seen that her first century is prelude to her second. The *Bowdoin* now enjoys recognition as a United States Historical Landmark, and as the State of Maine Official Vessel, there will continue to be support for her maintenance, including her current endowment. Authorized as a USCG Certified Sail Training Vessel to enhance her mission, as well as having those eager to fulfill it with the students, faculty, and leadership of Maine Maritime Academy, the *Bowdoin* remains an incomparable sailing vessel, as well as an indisputable educational asset.

# ACKNOWLEDGMENTS

THIS BOOK COULD NOT HAVE BEEN COMPLETED WITHOUT THE assistance of my colleagues and the *Bowdoin*'s captains, especially Captain Will McLean. He updated notes, made appropriate corrections, and generously gave time, original photographs, and detailed observations on the *Bowdoin,* past and present. The schooner is in good hands.

Thanks to my manuscript reviewers, Anne Romans, the director of the Witherlee Library, and Michael Joyce, the host of the WERU program "Boat Talk." Appreciation for clarity in technical support to Joseph Cullen and inspiring advice to Tom Koerner. Thanks to my editor, Michael Steere, for his assistance.

My thanks to Mark and Izzy.

# NOTES

## CHAPTER 1

1. Everett S. Allen, *Arctic Odyssey* (New York: Dodd, Mead and Company, 1962), 221.
2. Manuscript found in the Donald Baxter MacMillan Collection, Bowdoin College Library, Bowdoin College, Brunswick, Maine.
3. Allen, *Arctic Odyssey,* 147.
4. Ibid., 43.
5. Ibid., 44.
6. Ibid., 53.
7. Ibid., 56.
8. Ibid., 59.
9. Ibid., 60.
10. Ibid., 221.
11. Ibid.
12. Ibid., 222.
13. Ibid.
14. Ibid., 223.
15. James P. Delagado, *Bowdoin National Historical Landmark Study* (Washington DC: National Park Service: Marine Heritage Program, 1989), 3, Section 7.
16. Allen, *Arctic Odyssey,* 223.
17. Ibid.
18. Delagado, *Bowdoin National Historical Landmark Study,* 2, Section 7.
19. Allen, *Arctic Odyssey,* 223.
20. Captain William D. McLean, interviews in December 2020 by the author.
21. Allen, *Artic Odyssey,* 223.
22. Ibid.
23. Audrey Hodgdon, interviews in October 2020.
24. Mary Morton Cowan, *Captain Mac* (Honesdale, PA: Boyds Mills Press, 2010), 92.
25. Donald Baxter MacMillan, *Etah and Beyond* (New York: Houghton Mifflin Company, 1927), 43.
26. Ibid.
27. Allen, *Arctic Odyssey,* 224.
28. Cowan, *Captain Mac,* 179.

29. Ibid., 168.
30. MacMillan, *Etah and Beyond*, 68.
31. Ibid., Dedication Page.
32. Ibid., 60.
33. Allen, *Arctic Odyssey*, 226.
34. Ibid., 227.
35. Ibid.
36. Ibid.
37. Ibid., 228.
38. Ibid.
39. Ibid., 230.
40. Ibid., 231.
41. Ibid.
42. Ibid., 238.

## CHAPTER 2

1. Donald Baxter MacMillan, *Etah and Beyond*, (New York: Houghton Mifflin Company, 1927), 5.
2. Ibid., 12.
3. Ibid., 60.
4. Ibid., 97.
5. Ibid., 102.
6. Ibid., 115.
7. Ibid., 120.
8. Ibid., 123.
9. Ibid., 124.
10. Ibid., 214.
11. Ibid., 216.
12. Ibid., 217.
13. Ibid., 218.
14. Ibid., 219.
15. Ibid.
16. Ibid., 247.
17. Ibid., 248.
18. Ibid.
19. Ibid.
20. Ibid.
21. Donald Baxter MacMillan, *The Bowdoin in Baffin Land* (Unpublished Manuscript), Bowdoin Special Collections, Bowdoin College Library, Bowdoin College, Brunswick, Maine.

22. Everett S. Allen, *Arctic Odyssey* (New York: Dodd, Mead and Company, 1962), 50.
23. Ibid., 271.
24. MacMillan, *Etah and Beyond*, Foreword, xix.
25. Allen, *Arctic Odyssey*, 270.
26. Ibid., 273.
27. Ibid., 274.
28. Ibid., 271.
29. Ibid., 275.
30. Ibid., 275.
31. Ibid., 280.
32. Ibid.
33. Miriam L. MacMillan, *Green Seas and White Ice* (New York: Dodd, Mead, 1948), 249.
34. Allen, *Arctic Odyssey*, 285.
35. Ibid., 289.
36. Ibid., 294.
37. Ibid., 293.
38. Ibid., 294.
39. Ibid., 285.
40. Virginia Thorndike, *The Arctic Schooner Bowdoin: A Biography* (Unity, ME: North Country Press, 1995), 102.
41. Ibid., 119.
42. Ibid., 130.
43. Ibid., 132.
44. Ibid.
45. Ibid.
46. Ibid., 105.
47. Ibid.
48. Ibid.
49. Ibid., 106.
50. Ibid., 110.
51. Ibid., 111.
52. Allen, *Arctic Odyssey*, 291.
53. Ibid., 292.
54. Ibid., 294.
55. Ibid.
56. Thorndike, *The Arctic Schooner Bowdoin*, 119.
57. Ibid., 120.
58. Ibid., 122.
59. Allen, *Arctic Odyssey*, 298.

60. Ibid.
61. Ibid., 304.
62. Ibid., 305.
63. Ibid., 306.

## CHAPTER 3

1. Mary Morton Cowan, *Captain Mac* (Honesdale, PA: Boyds Mills Press, 2010), 176.
2. Ibid., 187.
3. Ibid., 188.
4. Everett S. Allen, *Arctic Odyssey* (New York: Dodd, Mead and Company, 1962), 303.
5. Ibid., 297.
6. Ibid., 304.
7. Ibid., 302.
8. Cowan, *Captain Mac,* 172.
9. Ibid., 176.
10. Ibid., 171.
11. Ibid., 179.
12. Allen, *Arctic Odyssey,* 311.
13. Ibid., 312.
14. Ibid.
15. Ibid.

## CHAPTER 4

1. Dr. Edward Morse, quoted in Virginia Thorndike, *The Arctic Schooner* Bowdoin*: A Biography* (Unity, ME: North Country Press, 1995).
2. Ibid.
3. D. B. MacMillan, quoted in A.S. Horr, *The Log of the Schooner* Bowdoin (Cleveland: World, 1947), Preface.
4. Everett S. Allen, *Artic Odyssey* (New York: Dodd, Mead and Company, 1962), 329.
5. Tennyson, Alfred Lord. *Sir John Franklin's Memorial,* 487.
6. Virginia Thorndike, *The Arctic Schooner* Bowdoin*: A Biography* (Unity, ME: North Country Press, 1995), 138.
7. Ibid., 141.
8. Ibid., 143.
9. Ibid., 144.
10. Ibid.
11. Ibid.

12. Ibid., 145.
13. Ibid.
14. Ibid., 146.
15. Ibid.
16. Ibid.
17. Ibid., 147.
18. Ibid., 149.
19. Ibid., 153.
20. Ibid., 158.
21. Ibid.
22. Ibid., 159.
23. Ibid., 161.
24. Ibid., 164.
25. Ibid.
26. Ibid.
27. Ibid., 165.
28. Ibid., 166.
29. Ibid.
30. Ibid.
31. Ibid.
32. Ibid., 168.

## CHAPTER 5

1. Virginia Thorndike, *The Arctic Schooner* Bowdoin: *A Biography* (Unity, ME: North Country Press, 1995), 169.
2. Ibid.
3. Ibid., 179.
4. Ibid.
5. Ibid., 171.
6. Ibid.
7. Ibid., 173.
8. Ibid.
9. Ibid.
10. Ibid., 177.
11. Ibid.
12. Ibid.
13. Ibid.
14. Ibid.
15. Ibid.
16. Ibid.

## CHAPTER 6

1. Brenda Lange, ed, *Sail Tall Ships! A Directory of Adventure and Education under Sail,* 23rd edition (Newport, RI: Tall Ships America, 2020), 113.
2. Cate Cronin, *Notes on Outward Bound,* October–November 2020.
3. Hurricane Island Outward Bound School, *Aboard a Living Legend: The Schooner* Bowdoin. (Camden, ME: Outward Bound School Program, 1987), 2.
4. Cronin, *Notes,* 1P, 1.
5. Ibid.
6. Ibid.
7. Ibid.
8. Ibid.
9. Ibid.
10. Cronin, telephone interview, April 2020.
11. Ibid.
12. Hurricane Island Outward Bound School, *HIOBS* Bowdoin *Program*, 3.
13. Cronin, telephone interviews by the author, May 2020.
14. Cronin, *Notes,* 1.
15. Ibid., 2.
16. Ibid.
17. Hurricane Island Outward Bound, *HIOBS* Bowdoin *Program*, 2.
18. Ibid., 2.
19. Cronin, *Notes,* 2.
20. Cronin, telephone interviews, October 2020.
21. Ibid.

## CHAPTER 7

1. Virginia Thorndike, . *The Arctic Schooner* Bowdoin: *A Biography* (Unity, ME: North Country Press, 1995), 186.
2. Cate Cronin, quoted in Thorndike, *The Arctic Schooner* Bowdoin: *A Biography*, 186.
3. Thorndike, *The Arctic Schooner* Bowdoin: *A Biography*, 186.
4. Ibid.
5. Ibid., 187.
6. Ibid.
7. Ibid., 188.
8. Ibid.
9. Ibid., 189.
10. Ibid.
11. Ibid.
12. Ibid.
13. Ibid., 192.

14. Ibid., 193.
15. Ibid.
16. Ibid., 190.
17. Ibid.
18. Andy Chase, quoted in Brown, "North to Labrador," *Down East* (August 1991), 37.
19. James P. Delagado, "*Bowdoin* Natural Historic Landmark Study," National Park Service, Maritime Heritage Program.
20. Thorndike, *The Arctic Schooner* Bowdoin: *A Biography,* 194.

## CHAPTER 8

1. Virginia Thorndike, *The Arctic Schooner* Bowdoin: *A Biography* (Unity, ME: North Country Press, 1995), 195.
2. Ibid.
3. Ibid.
4. Ibid.
5. Ibid., 197.
6. Ibid.
7. Ibid., 198.
8. Ibid.
9. Ibid.
10. Ibid., 199.
11. Ibid.
12. Ibid., 200.
13. Ibid., 201.
14. Ibid.
15. Ibid., 203.
16. Ibid.
17. Ibid.
18. Ibid., 204.
19. Ibid., 209.
20. Ibid., 211.
21. Ibid.
22. Ibid., 212.
23. Ibid., 214.
24. Ibid., 221.
25. Ibid., 223.
26. Ibid., 227.
27. Ibid.
28. Ibid., 228.
29. Ibid., 229.

30. Ibid., 230.
31. Ibid., 232.
32. Ibid., 236.
33. Ibid., 238.
34. Ibid.
35. Ibid.
36. Ibid.
37. Ibid., 241.
38. Ibid., 248.
39. Ibid., 231.
40. Ibid., 250.
41. Ibid., 251.
42. Elliot Rappaport, "70 Degrees North," *The Mariner* (Winter, 1995–1996), 11.
43. Ibid.
44. Ibid.
45. Thorndike, *The Arctic Schooner* Bowdoin*: A Biography*, 255.
46. Rappaport, "70 Degrees North," 11.
47. Ibid.
48. Ibid.
49. Sid Clemens, quoted in Thorndike, *The Arctic Schooner* Bowdoin*: A Biography*, 255.
51. Jim Sharp, ed., "Captains Quarters," You Tube Presentation, January 12, 2021.

## CHAPTER 9

1. Elliot Rappaport, *The Mariner,* Issue 2 (1996), 10.
2. Ibid.
3. Ibid., 11.
4. William McLean, *The Mariner,* Issue 2 (2019), 9.
5. Ibid.
6. Ibid.
7. Ibid.
8. William McLean, interview with author, December 2020.
9. Jack Frazier, conversation with author, December 2017.
10. Eric Romelczyk, quoted in William McLean, *CR – 214 Course* (Castine, ME: Maine Maritime Academy, 2020), 2.
11. William McLean, interview with author, December 2020.
12. Andy Chase, quoted in Brenda Lange, ed. *Sail Tall Ships! A Directory of Adventure and Education under Sail*, 23rd edition (Newport, RI: Tall Ships America, 2020), 30.

13. Ibid.
14. William McLean, interview with author, December 2020.
15. Eric Jergensen, elective offered fall 2020 (Castine, ME: Maine Maritime Academy).
16. Ibid.
17. Ibid.
18. Ibid.
19. MARAD, 2017.
20. John Murray, "Port Director's Perspective," *The Mariner*, Issue 3 (2019), 38.
21. Ibid.
22. The Decade of Ocean Literacy (2021–2030) declared by the United Nations, June 2020, at New York, New York.

## CHAPTER 10

1. Kenneth Curtis, quoted in James R. Aldrich, *Fair Winds and Stormy Seas* (Stonington, ME: Penobscot Press, 1991).
2. Maine Maritime Academy College Catalogue, Castine, ME, 2020.
3. William McLean, interview with the author, December 2020.
4. Ibid.

## CHAPTER 11

1. Donald Baxter MacMillan, *Etah and Beyond or Life within 12 Degrees of the Pole* (New York: Houghton Mifflin Company, 1927), 80.
2. Aaron Grainik, quoted in William McLean, *CR – 214 Course*, 2.
3. William McLean, interview with the author, December 2020.
4. William R. Sims, ed., "Bowdoin Sails into the Future." *The Mariner,* Issue 1 (2020), 10.
5. Ibid.
6. Ibid.
7. Andy Chase, "Bowdoin Centennial Campaign." *The Mariner,* Issue 1 (2015), 34.
8. Ibid.
9. Ibid.
10. Janet Acker, The Minutes of the Board of Trustees Meeting of Maine Maritime Academy. 2020.
11. William McLean, interview with the author, December 2020.

## EPILOGUE

1. Tennyson, Alfred Lord. *Ulysses*, 1842.

# BIBLIOGRAPHY

Allen, Everett S. *Arctic Odyssey: The Life of Rear Admiral Donald B. MacMillan.* New York: Dodd, Mead and Company, 1962.

Brown, James P. "North to Labrador," *Down East,* August 1991.

Chase, Andy. Emails, 2020.

Cowan, Mary Morton. *Captain Mac: The Life of Donald Baxter MacMillan, Arctic Explorer.* Honesdale, PA: Calkins Creek, 2010.

Cronin, Cate. *Notes on Outward Bound.* October 2020.

Cronin, Cate. Telephone interviews by the author, April–October 2020.

Delagado, James P. "*Bowdoin* National Historic Study." National Park Service, Marine Heritage Program. Washington, DC, 1989.

Gayman, Amy. "The Coast Guard's Challenges in the Arctic." *Proceedings.* Vol. 77, No. 1 (Spring, 2020): 24–29.

Hodgdon, Audrey. Telephone conversations, September–December 2020.

A. S. Horr, *The Log of the Schooner Bowdoin.* Cleveland: World, 1947.

Hurricane Island Outward Bound School. *Aboard a Living Legend, The Schooner Bowdoin.* Camden, ME: Outward Bound School Program, 1987.

Lange, Brenda, ed. *Sail Tall Ships! A Directory of Adventure and Education under Sail,* 23rd Edition. Newport, RI: Tall Ships America, 2020.

MacMillan, Donald Baxter. *Etah and Beyond, or Life within 12 Degrees of the Pole.* New York: Houghton Mifflin Company, 1927.

MacMillan, Donald Baxter. *Four Years in the White North.* New York: Harper, 1918.

MacMillan, Donald Baxter. Unpublished Manuscript: *The Bowdoin in Baffin Land.* Donald Baxter MacMillan Collection, Bowdoin College Library, Bowdoin College, Brunswick, ME.

MacMillan, Miriam L. *Green Seas and White Ice.* New York: Dodd, Mead, 1948.

McLean, William. Interviews by the author, December 2020.

Murray, John. "Port Director's Perspective." *The Mariner.* Issue 3, 2019.

Pundt, Ralph. Telephone interview with the author, December 2020.

Rolfe, W. J., ed. *Tennyson.* Boston: Houghton Mifflin Company, 1898.

Rappaport, Elliot. "70 Degrees North: Maine Maritime in the Arctic." *Mariner,* 1995–1996.

Sharp, Jim. "Captains Quarters." Youtube Presentation. The Sail, Steam and Power Museum, Camden, ME. January 12, 2021.

Sims, William, ed. Castine, ME: *The Mariner,* 2015–2020.

Spectre, Peter H. "The *Bowdoin* Project." *Wooden Boat,* July/August 1982.

Stackpole, Renny. "The Saga of the Arctic Schooner *Bowdoin.*" *Sea History,* Summer, 1986.

Thorndike, Virginia. *The Arctic Schooner* Bowdoin*: A Biography.* Unity, ME: North Country Press, 1995.

Willis, Dana. Telephone interviews by the author, September, December 2020.

# INDEX

# AUTHOR'S NOTE

THIS BOOK BEGAN AS A STUDY ON AN EDUCATIONAL SAILING VESsel and her historic importance as a long-standing example of ocean literacy. As described by contemporary author John Fowles, the venerable term "ship" is reserved for vessels that venture into the unknown, such as spaceships. This designation, he maintains, is indicative of "a greater value on outward line than on soul or utility, and nowhere more than with the last of the sailing ships, that splendidly and sharply individualized the zenith of five thousand years of hard-earned knowledge and aesthetic instinct . . . space- and starships . . . yet when man really reaches, across the vast seas of space, he still reaches in ships. Other words may function as well; no other has the poetries."

As research commenced, I was informed, and subsequently found that many discrepancies in each of the earlier books on the schooner needed be reconciled. To this end, documentation would most effectively illustrate the *Bowdoin*'s voyages and history by the captains who skippered her in her first 100 years. The study became a volume of interesting sailing history, and the importance of the *Bowdoin*'s role in the record of Northern expeditions and as an historical example reflects the current status of exploration as the future of the Arctic region opens.

# ABOUT THE AUTHOR

Kathryn A. Beals is the author of *Thinking Through Writing*, a study in critical thinking using maritime literature for instruction in an example of a maritime college writing course. Translated into more than a dozen languages, the text emphasizes writing as the most effective learning tool, in any academic area on any educational level, due to the brain's visual orientation. *The Arctic Schooner Bowdoin: One Hundred Years of Wind, Sea, and Ice* is the author's second book, advocating the importance of sail in maritime training and the seaworthiness of the historic wooden schooner *Bowdoin* as an enduring educational example. A book on ocean literacy is forthcoming.